P9-CEQ-125

Contents

ACKNOWLEDGMENTS

To the many friends who made *Forgotten Girls* possible, we offer our deepest gratitude. Affiliate and sister ministry leaders opened their hearts, shared hundreds of ministry hours with us and introduced us to the girls in this book. Without their willingness to share so generously, we could not have completed the book. Many of the ministries work under oppression and asked that we not acknowledge them by name, so we honor them with thanksgiving to God. To those we can acknowledge, we openly give our thanks: Bible Faith Mission, Center for Legal Aid, Assistance and Settlement of Pakistan, Elam of Iran, Oasis India, InterSenegal Mission, Peace Rehabilitation Center of Nepal, Smart Heart of Egypt, and Grace International Ministries of Japan.

Most of the research for the book was garnered by the dedicated international team at Sisters In Service. Our gratitude goes to Katherine Anderson, Cherylann Sammons, Pauline Y., Melissa Eisenbrandt, Esther Vukosavovic, Pam Pitt, Bob Morrison, and their boss, Daniel Rickett (Michele Rickett's husband). Daniel receives double acknowledgment, along with Kay's husband, Dan Kline. Our husbands once again lovingly encouraged us to travel and invest the time we needed to write.

Four years ago Cindy Bunch, editor at InterVarsity Press, began talking to us about a book to follow *Daughters of Hope*. She enthusiastically encouraged us to focus on the lives of girls around the world. Her patience and coaching were invaluable.

We offer our deep gratitude to the hundreds of supporters and praying advocates who believed in this book even before it was written. They saw by faith that their prayers and sacrifice would raise the awareness and ongoing support to restore the lives of hurting girls.

The women and girls we interviewed, who entrusted their stories of pain, dignity and courage have our love and thanks forever. The book is dedicated not just to the girls who stories we tell, but also to the millions of others who suffer along with them. If our work can somehow raise awareness and help for them, we are most grateful to God.

Introduction

Have you ever noticed how seldom something "life changing" really changes your life? The term gets tossed around a lot—to describe watching the sun set in a gorgeous blaze of color, for instance, or to rave about an exciting adventure. Consider the number of books with the phrase splashed across the front cover. Good things, all. Inspiring and helpful and memorable. But *life changing?*

Yet truly life-changing events do occur. Events that forever mark a divide between the *then* and *now* of life. Between despair and hope. Between ignorance and understanding. Between death and life.

Consider Parimala. She barely had time to draw her first breath before she experienced a life-changing event. As her mother staggered in from the fields, the baby was already entering the world. But no one rejoiced in her birth. When her father saw that the baby was a girl, he grabbed her up and carried her outside. He dug a hole in the hard ground beside their thatch-roofed hut and dropped her in. Then he covered her with dirt.

Done, and done.

But the baby's grandfather saw it all. And he knew that every night for the rest of his life that baby's accusing wail would echo up from the ground to torment him and haunt his sleep. So while his son sat at the table eating his dinner and as his daughter-in-law wept in the corner, the old man crept outside and dug the baby out of the hole. He carried her choking and gasping to a nearby medical clinic, where he laid her down by the door. Then he headed back home, confident that he would sleep in peace.

Inside the clinic, the nurse stopped sorting papers and cocked her head to listen. The sound was faint, but . . . yes, it was definitely a choking gasp, and it was just outside the door. When she poked her head out to investigate, she saw the infant lying on the rocky ground, struggling to breathe, her nose and mouth clogged with dirt. Already the tiny, gasping face showed a blue tinge. The nurse sighed and shook her head. Then she went back inside, picked up the telephone receiver and called a couple who ran an orphanage for boys.

"It's a girl," she stated matter-of-factly. "She will not last long. If you want her, come quickly." Then she hung up and went back to sorting papers.

That's how little Parimala entered the world.

Welcome, sweet baby. You have plenty of company, for little girls are tossed away every day. Many who manage to survive are exploited, abused, neglected and oppressed—so many little ones who will never know they are God's precious treasures.

Unless, that is, life-changing events intersect their lives.

On that first day of Parimala's life, the couple who ran the orphanage hurried over to the clinic in response to the nurse's call. They plucked the newborn off the ground and quickly cleared the dirt from her nose and mouth. Then they wrapped her in a cloth and carried her home with them, telling her all the way what a precious treasure she was. That day they stepped into the gap on her behalf and changed her life.

Just as it has always been everywhere around the world, today the defenseless and powerless suffer most. And who is more defenseless than a child? Who more powerless than a girl, written off as worthless and expendable?

Unwanted.

A burden.

A curse.

Such is the heritage of multitudes born into the belt of nations that extends from West Africa all the way to Asia—home to the least educated, to those with the least access to health care, to the poorest members of the poorest countries on earth. Look closely at the world's most oppressed, and you will find them to be overwhelmingly female. Indeed, women and children make up

- 80 percent of the world's refugees.
- 70 percent of the poorest of the poor.
- two-thirds of the world's illiterate.
- four million annual victims of human traffickers.
- 80 percent of those who have never heard of Jesus Christ.

FOCUSING ON GIRLS

Around the world, women suffer from myriad problems that keep them oppressed and locked in poverty. But more and more we are finding that many of these adult problems actually develop in childhood. So if we are to have the greatest possible impact on women in the generations to come, it is imperative that we double our efforts toward today's young ones. They are the nurturers of the future. They are the heart of tomorrow's homes.

Girls born into a life of abandonment and abuse, resented and oppressed from birth, grow up acting out their oppression and abandonment. They believe they truly *are* inferior and deserving of abuse. Unless a life-changing event interrupts this pattern, abused and oppressed girls grow up to be abused and oppressed women.

When we met Parimala, she was an apple-cheeked two-year-old with dancing brown eyes and a bubbly personality. Kay gave her a Hershey's Kiss, the first chocolate she had ever tasted. Parimala rolled the tasty treat around on her tongue, and her eyes sparkled. As the Kiss began to melt, a chocolaty smile spread across her face. Parimala jumped for joy and hugged our knees—but only so long as her auntie and uncle were in sight.

Auntie and Uncle changed Parimala's life by bringing her into their house, where they accepted and loved her as their own. Curious neighbors peered over the fence to see this couple who actually *chose* a girl. They watched as Auntie cared for her and sang as she fed the child from her own plate. They watched as Uncle tenderly rocked her and carried her with him when he went out to check the cows.

In time, the bolder among them came right out and asked, "A *girl*? Why would you waste time and money on a girl?" That was a question they loved to answer, for it gave them a chance to affirm the value of every girl and every girl's right to live. Again and again the couple repeated that girls are made in God's image too, and are also precious in his sight.

The neighbors didn't have too much to say, but evidently they listened. No baby girl is known to have been buried alive in that village since Parimala.

Rescue. Restoration. Prevention. These are the steps to real change.

If a newborn buried alive by her father in India can have a future, why not a tossed-away girl in Tibet or Mali or China? Why not a forgotten child in Japan or a girl trafficked and sold in Nepal? Why not a little one languishing in Sudan or Iran or Iraq? We are convinced that every unwanted girl has the potential of a different ending to her story.

On the way out of India, we passed the time in the Bangalore airport, thumbing through an Indian newspaper. A short article ended with these sobering sentences: "Look into a child's eyes, and where we should see innocence and hope, we see hunger, fear, suspicion. We need to take a look at the society we have created."

Too often we judge our progress as a society by what we have accumulated. Material goods, money, homes—all the things we think mark us as successful. If we really want to catch a glimpse of where we are headed, we will do well to look at how we treat the most tender and vulnerable among us—and how we allow others to treat them. This is a far better indicator of our chances of surviving and thriving in the generations to come.

RESIST THE DARKNESS

Altogether, our work in international ministry spans over thirty years and covers dozens of countries, from Latin America across Africa to the Middle East to Asia. Michele lived and worked in East Africa in the 1980s, and every year since has traveled in developing countries to create relationships and to research and evaluate women's projects. Kay, a full-time writer, has worked in fourteen countries in conjunction with writing projects and speaking engagements.

Everywhere we've been in the developing world, we have seen women and girls endure the uneven weight of every imaginable kind of burden. We've seen them shamelessly abused and exploited. And we have seen them endure all kinds of sufferings with amazing dignity.

It is a fact that women and girls around the globe suffer more than men and boys. Sisters In Service (SIS), the Christian not-for-profit organization Michele founded, was formed expressly to garner and share the most current research on the plight of women in developing nations and to provide interventions for those women.

Because empowering women makes them less vulnerable to oppression and exploitation, we began by raising awareness and advocacy and by developing ways to strengthen and restore women's lives. This brought us in contact with courageous women and men already addressing the needs of women and children in the hardest places.

Powerful interventions require linking arms over the long haul and together growing good initiatives into great ones. The best way to do this is to identify local ministries that already work well. Local women have profound insight into the cultural forces in their homeland that lead to oppression and exploitation. They understand how to do things in a way that works in their area, that are cost-effective and that won't draw the backlash that can crush an effort. It is they, after all, who will live with the consequences.

So we began by looking for local ministries with which we shared mutual goals, ministries that have proven leadership, integrity, effectiveness and growth potential. They already have their role. Our role is of a supportive servant: we advocate, consult and provide resource and learning opportunities.

Each time either of us traveled, we came home enriched and inspired by the lives of courage, faith and faithfulness of the women we met. And each time we told their stories, people wanted to know more. Our first book, *Daughters of Hope,* tells the stories of women who suffer to serve God in the most difficult circumstances.

As we continued to look for the most effective ways to battle abuse and exploitation, everything pointed toward little girls. For when girls grow up undervalued, underfed, illiterate, physically abused and exploited, the generations that come after them are destined to groan under waves of evil. So if we ever hope to see change in the way women are treated, we absolutely must focus our efforts on stopping the abuse of little girls. That is exactly what we at SIS are doing, particularly in our national initiative "Resist the Darkness" (see page 176).

We know God hears the cries of the weak, and we know he answers them. Job, who knew all about suffering, wrote, "But those who suffer he delivers in their suffering; he speaks to them in their affliction" (Job 36:15). As you read these stories, we hope you will see God's love reaching into every young life.

Like all children everywhere, these girls have their own "normal." Because they have not seen any world other than the one in which they live, they have no idea what life is like elsewhere. We talked to girls in Nepal, sold to sex traffickers by their parents, who could not comprehend what it means to be loved. To girls in Sudan who could not fathom life without war. To girls in India who had no understanding of their value. To girls all over who had no concept of being satisfied by a meal or saving money for the future or going outside simply to play, because normal life means hunger and want and endless work.

Yet we also saw within these girls a wonderful potential to bring about change in the families they themselves would be raising in very few years. And if their families change, imagine the effect that will have on their villages. And then the effect their villages will have on the larger communities. And if enough communities are changed, imagine how that will affect entire countries.

Little girls like Parimala can change the world!

It is both a blessing and a challenge for us to record these stories. People ask us how we are able to get interviews with girls in so many difficult places. In most cases, we have established relationships through our ongoing work with women. Some of our hosts for these interview trips are long-term partners, though not all.

Because most live in hostile places, we must guard their identities. All the accounts in this book are true. The people are real; the stories are factual. We have changed names and identifying details, however; this we must do because of the sensitive nature involved in so many of the situations and locations. Occasionally we have combined several stories to make the narrative easier for readers to follow. But in all cases, each element of the story is factual. Likewise, except for the photo of Yoshi in Japan, the photographs in each chapter were taken by our team or ministry friends to represent girls in the country that each chapter discusses.

On television, we see the faces of hungry children and little ones who wander through war-torn villages. But to really understand the raw ugliness of oppression and poverty, Western Christians need to get to know real individuals. We decided to help you do exactly that: we bring the stories to you, not just to inform you, but so that you can be part of the solution, so that we can work together to obey the words of God as recorded by the prophet Isaiah:

Seek justice,
    encourage the oppressed.
Defend the cause of the fatherless,
    plead the case of the widow. (Isaiah 1:17)

Come along with us and meet the girls of the world.

Yes, you will encounter suffering. But don't turn away because of the pain. Beyond the abuse and oppression, past the awfulness and neglect, you will catch glimpses of glorious dignity and staggering resilience, of remarkable potential and untold value. In these girls you will see the sparkle of hope and the promise of the future.

It is our prayer that meeting these girls will be a life-changing event for you. We hope that by the time you finish this book, you will be compelled to seek out the way God would have you be involved in the care of "the least of these," your sisters.

PART 1

PHYSICAL LIFE

*I*n a mountain village in southern China, a six-year-old bitten by a snake on the way to school waited three days for the car that transports people to the closest medical facility, two hours away. Just before the car arrived, the child died.

Illness and accidents take on a whole new face for those who live in the hardest places of the world. When medical care is scarce, every problem—even a treatable one—can quickly become a disaster.

Where people lack access to clean drinking water or basic sanitation, the situation is particularly dire. Diseases such as malaria and cholera easily reach epidemic proportions. And something as commonplace as a bout of diarrhea can be a death sentence.

Girls are at an even greater risk than boys because, from babyhood, girls consistently get the short end of the nutritional stick. Frequently girls are the last in the family to eat, so they get whatever is left, which means they often have little protein in their diets. The result is that many exist in a state of precarious health, which translates into a higher mortality rate for girls. And many families who will do whatever it takes to get medical help for their sick or injured boys, leave their girls to struggle along with home remedies. The value of a girl to the family simply is not as great as the value of a boy.

Many children in these areas of concern also suffer due to the AIDS epidemic. In China, in India, in country after country across Africa, children are afflicted. Others, left orphaned by the disease, struggle to survive any way they can. In sub-Saharan Africa, where in the fifteen-to-twenty-four age group two girls are infected for every infected boy, half the girls believe the myth that a healthy-looking person cannot carry the virus. In the most-affected areas, five or six adolescent girls are infected for every infected boy.

According to some reports, close to one quarter of the girls in India die before they ever reach the ripe old age of sixteen.

Yet the lack of physical welfare goes beyond malnutrition and the well-documented plagues in poverty-afflicted areas. Most frightful of all is the physical harm purposely and systematically inflicted on girls. In places least-reached with the gospel, it is a daunting challenge to many little ones simply to be allowed to come into the world alive—especially in China and India, home to more than a third of the world's six billion people.

According to UNICEF, gender-based infanticide, abortion, malnutrition and neglect are believed to be behind sixty to one hundred million women "missing" from the world's population.

In this section we will explore some of the lesser-known physical needs of girls and what is being done to help them.

1

Stand Up to the Witch

Indonesia

*T*he first time Michele saw the preschooler with the choppy haircut, she bent down to give the child a warm, face-to-face greeting. Michele couldn't tell if she was talking to a boy or a girl. With her Indonesian friend Mirah translating, Michele smiled and stroked the child's hair.

"Look closely," Mirah said as she brushed the child's hair aside. Long scars crisscrossed the little head. Mirah continued, "The one who brought this child in exclaimed, 'Just look! Someone cut her head with scissors.'" Then Mirah pulled up the child's sleeve to reveal burn and slash scars. "Every part of her body except her face and hands is covered with scars."

Michele could not hide her horror. After the child had slipped away, she demanded, "Who did this to her?"

Mirah told us Beti's story.

Beti was not quite four years old when her mother left her with a neighbor. She was going to find Beti's father and bring him home, and she promised to be back in two weeks to get her child. When several months passed and Beti's mother did not return, the neighbor began asking people in the village if someone would take the child into their home.

Immediately a woman eagerly agreed—Borang, the local witch doctor. Her own daughter had given birth to a son, she said, and with so many people in their house, they needed a babysitter and house-keeper. Beti could work in exchange for room and board.

But the child was far too young for such duties. Everyone in the village knew that. Even so, and although they feared for Beti, no one would argue with the fearsome witch. Her abilities to call on dark forces to intervene in peoples' lives were infamous. Anyone who crossed her paid a heavy price.

Borang lived in a wooden house with two rooms. The front room was for eating and for meeting with customers. It was dark and smoky, with a low ceiling and dirt floor. Against the walls stood rough, filthy tables piled high with pots, jars and boxes containing ingredients for her "magic." Drying herbs hung from the ceiling alongside rodent carcasses.

In the back room, the family slept on two mattresses. When little Beti was "good," she was allowed to sleep inside the house on the dirt floor in the front room. Most nights, however, she was tied to a tree in the backyard.

One day, the witch yelled out from the house, "Beti, you misera-ble dog!" The little girl knew from painful experience to run in and quietly receive yet another punishment for yet another offense she didn't understand.

The witch was waiting just inside the door. She slapped Beti so hard her ear rang, then she scolded, "This plate is still dirty!"

The witch grabbed Beti's arm and shook her, then hurried her toward the back room, where the cruelest punishments were ex-acted. First came the cigarette burns, then the cuttings on her arms, legs and bottom. Beti tried not to cry loudly. Drawing atten-tion to the house only brought more punishments. Sometimes she accidentally wet herself, and then she was beaten again for making a mess.

The witch even cut Beti under her hair, where she thought no one would see the wounds. But the blood ran down the little girl's face and neck, and since she was never bathed, her hair matted with blood and dirt, and her skin developed a crusty layer of mud and oozing sores.

The neighbor next door saw the child's suffering, and it disgusted her. When she could no longer stand to hear Beti crying for her mother, she pleaded with Borang to let the little girl go. The neighbor even plucked up her courage and threatened to call the police. Borang ignored her. One day, fearing the witch would kill Beti, the neighbor actually did call the police. But to Borang's delight, they had no interest in a worthless girl. They never even came by.

As time went on and Beti stayed with the witch, she grew to act like a wild animal. She never spoke. When anyone came near her, she would only whimper.

More than once, the neighbors raised concerns about the child to the village leaders. But no one knew what to do. They could not move Beti to another house in the village, because the witch would certainly retaliate. Then someone suggested they send the child to the new preschool at the Christian seminary. Perhaps the leader—Mirah—would have an idea of someone in her area who would want Beti.

So the next-door neighbor was sent to Mirah with an urgent message about an abused girl badly in need of help. Mirah came immediately and went with a few neighbors to the witch's backyard. As she examined the little girl's wounds and scars, she seethed with anger.

"How did this happen?" she demanded.

Beti said little, for she trusted no one. But the people of the village gave Mirah more than enough to let her know she must take action.

"Let's have a talk with this witch," Mirah said. Without hesitation, she led the neighbors to the woman's house.

"We would like to help Beti become like other little girls," Mirah told the witch.

Borang spit an unintelligible reply at them and roughly grabbed the little girl's arm in an attempt to pull her inside. But Mirah's hand moved quickly, resting firmly on top of the witch's hand.

"If you cannot take better care of Beti, we can find someone who will," Mirah said. "I will be watching to see if the child improves. If not, I will be back to talk with you."

The door slammed in their faces, and they could hear the witch's angry voice fading toward the back room.

A week later, Beti was found wandering in a daze down the dirt road that bisects the village. Never before had anyone seen her off the witch's property. But here the child was, stumbling along with what appeared to be a rag on top of her head, seemingly blind to the world. As they looked more closely, they could see that the child's head had been laid open by large gashes. Her filthy clothes were covered with fresh blood.

That was it. The neighbors rushed Beti to the village leaders. They worked on bandaging Beti's head while the next-door neighbor hurried back to Mirah with a message.

When the neighbor arrived at the seminary and explained Beti's condition, Mirah's face flooded with angry tears. She sat down and wrote a contract naming Beti the ward of the seminary; the child would never return to the witch. Then Mirah went to meet with the villagers. She took the seminary's cook along and placed Beti in her loving care while she and the leaders went to see the witch.

"Half the village went to the witch's house with me," Mirah said. So she had plenty of support when she told Borang that her days of hurting Beti were over. "My hand was shaking as I shoved the contract toward her. I told her to sign the paper and to never again see the child."

"She is a lazy dog! Never could do any work!" the witch sneered. "I am glad to be rid of her. Give me the papers, and I'll sign."

The neighbors blinked at each other. They could not believe the witch would relinquish Beti so easily.

The first time we saw Beti, she had just been rescued. Now, after four years, we were eager to see her again. No longer a wild, frightened creature with chopped hair, she is now a gregarious young girl no one would mistake for a boy. She is the little sister of all the seminary students because she has been adopted by the cook who watched her that day four years ago. At every gathering, Beti begs to sing. She has a few favorites in her repertoire, and she eagerly performs them all, joyfully and courageously.

As we prepared to say goodbye, Beti busily puffed out a plastic bag, which she attached to a string.

"What are you making?" Michele asked her.

Beti offered to demonstrate. She skipped down the seminary driveway, then giggled triumphantly as her homemade parachute soared into the air.

2

Disposable Mothers

Tibet

Ten thousand feet above sea level, in the unforgiving corner of China known as the Qinghai-Tibetan Plateau, nomadic Tibetan tribes make a life where it seems impossible anyone could live. For half the year, the bleak landscape gets by with nothing more serious than droughts and sandstorms. But during the other six months, merciless winter storms pound the area with snow and hail, and bitter cold plunges the region to minus-thirty degrees—sometimes even lower.

Fifteen-year-old Sonam has never known life anywhere else. She hasn't seen a television or a car or a radio. She knows nothing of electricity. She doesn't understand the concept of time or of money, because she gets up with the sun and lies down when it is dark and because every exchange she has experienced has been on the barter system. As far back as Sonam can remember, she and her mother, Tenzing, have struggled to survive in a makeshift tent pieced together from tattered animal skins.

Tekunhu, that's what families such as Sonam's are called in the local language. It means "those who cannot survive without help." Certainly Sonam and her single mother fit into that category. In a land where agriculture is impossible (little will grow in such bitter conditions) and where danger constantly lurks (unforgiving weather threatens and hungry, wild animals prowl), almost every family head is a subsistence herder. Problem is, Tenzing doesn't own a single sheep or yak, so the only way she knows to feed herself and her daughter is to beg for food from others who themselves barely manage to survive. Sonam spends her days in a never-ending struggle to keep their tattered tent patched together. It is a job of vital importance, for without shelter, mother and daughter will be doomed.

"Why did you name me *Sonam?*" the girl asked her mother one stormy night as wind blew icy misery through the seams of the animal skins. "Why did you call me *fortunate one?* If I was fortunate, I would have been born a boy."

"Perhaps when you are reborn you will be a boy," Tenzing answered. It was the closest thing to hope she had to offer her daughter.

Tenzing had been Sonam's age when her father invited young men to come into their house and sleep with her. His hope was that she would get pregnant and add a boy to the family of girls. Her greatest contribution would be to raise another male hand to help him herd the family's livestock. But Tenzing had not borne a son. She'd had a daughter instead, which angered her father. Since none of the boys who had visited wanted to marry Tenzing, she was forced to join the ranks of the disposable mothers.

Farther out on the plateau, in a tiny mud shack not five feet high, sixteen-year-old Pema lived with her little brother and their sick mother. The shack served as a seasonal shelter for nomadic herdsmen and their yaks before Pema's desperate family moved in and claimed it for their own. All summer long it leaked, and when the freezing winds of winter came, the wet mud turned to ice. Since winter meant snowstorms and pounding hail, Pema's mother, Yangchen, worried that the shack would collapse around them. Were that to happen, it would leave the family fully exposed to the elements and ready prey for wild animals. In such a condition, none of them would survive the winter.

Yangchen, bent and weathered, leaned heavily on the stout stick that Pema had found for her, and she struggled to make her way outside the shelter. Aged and worn, she was not yet thirty-six years old.

"If we had a yak, we could have milk," Pema said wistfully. But they had no yak. So Pema and her brother spent another day searching for twigs they might sell as firewood.

Single mothers are all too common in this bitter climate, and their lot is often tragic. They occupy the lowest rung of society among China's Tibetan nomads. A husband might treat his wife terribly; he might beat her and force her to work hard all day and long into the night. But at least a married woman could boast that she had a man. And a married woman could work and earn a bit of money. Such was not possible for a woman alone. Not for a disposable mother.

Yangchen's husband had died five years earlier. His long illness used up everything the family owned. Yangchen even had to sell their small herd of yaks, a disaster for nomadic herders. She was left with nothing but a cooking pot and four bowls. Other women are alone because their husbands deserted them.

But many, like Tenzing, never married in the first place. This situation carries no stigma among the nomadic people. Children are considered legally mature at fifteen and are then free to choose mating partners. Marriage is optional, as long as both sides agree to the terms.

Some of these unions remain intact and some do not. When they don't, the mother keeps the children. Estimates suggest that 15 percent of the children born on the Qinghai-Tibetan Plateau are born to single mothers. When no family group is available to support a single woman and her children, she ends up at the mercy of her own devices, which for most women means next to no devices at all. Many become displaced, living in any shelter they can find—sometimes even just a hole in the ground. They and their children are caught up in an end-less struggle to survive from one day to the next.

In general, villages in the region claim a per capita income of less than 220 U.S. dollars per year. But the *Tekunhu*—the poorest of the poor—often do not get even half that much. Without outside help, most of these families would perish; no one would remember they ever existed. The Chinese government subsidizes each family with 110 pounds of flour and the equivalent of 2.40 U.S. dollars per year—precious little buffer between a family and starvation.

Needless to say, the idea of school never entered Sonam's mind. Why would it? Every resource she and her mother could scrape together, no matter how small, went for food and shelter. Families such as hers rivet their attention on just one thing: survival. They dare not waste energy on such frivolities as learning. Besides, if Sonam were to go to school, who would keep up with the constant tent repairs? Who would make certain their shelter didn't blow apart some stormy night, leaving her and her mother at the mercy of the killer cold?

Nor was school an option for Pema, or even for her brother. If Pema wasn't nursing her sick mother or trying to scrape up a bit of food, she was helping her brother search for wood to sell. Yet a day's hunt seldom yielded more than an armload of twigs and yak dung, about what was required for their own cooking fire.

Tekunhu are in such need of everything—food, heat, medical care, education, proper shelter—that it truly is difficult to know how to begin reaching out to them in a meaningful way. But of all their crush-ing needs, perhaps the most urgent is adequate shelter, for a house does much more than simply provide the family with protection from the cold and from wild animals. It also improves their health and, if they have a few animals, advances the livestock's health.

The impact of living in a real house truly can be life-changing. Children, freed from the endless job of repairing tattered tents or mud houses, can go to school. In some cases, a house has even allowed women to secure loans and start small businesses. It can literally lay the foundation for a new approach to life.

As we shared about the needs of so many Tibetan single mothers, donors provided for block homes to be built. Once a house is built, the local government furnishes the family with a stove, a stovepipe and a cooking pot, so a house also gives a mother a place to cook. And no one has to worry about the shelter falling down on them during a winter storm.

Sonam and her mother were the grateful recipients of one of these homes. Their first response? They decided that instead of inviting the boys in to see if Sonam could produce a son, she should go to school and learn to read and write. Sonam, they determined, would not be another *tekunhu*.

Sonam even looks different than she did last year. No longer is she skinny and gaunt; now her face is round and her cheeks a healthy pink. If you were to stop by their new, one-room house, you would likely find Tenzing boiling a pot of noodles for supper.

"Now we have food," Tenzing says. That's because the school sends its leftover food home with Sonam—whenever the school has leftover food, that is.

"See, Sonam?" Tenzing tells her daughter with a smile. "I did choose the right name for you! Sonam, you truly are the fortunate one."

For Pema, school was a more difficult decision. She agreed that her brother should attend but refused to go with him because she was reluctant to leave her mother alone. It was Yangchen who insisted, and although her body was frail, her spirit was strong. Should she not survive the winter—or the next or the next—Pema would have had no herds to sell, no extended family to fall back on.

Yangchen said to Pema, "You should not grow up the way I grew up, my daughter. You go to school and learn a better way."

So each morning Pema puts a little yak dung on the fire to ensure that her mother stays warm in the new house, then heads off to prepare herself for the future.

3

Sacrificed to Gods

India

*T*oday is a day of blessing!" That's what everyone shouted as the June festival celebrations began.

And a day of blessing is exactly what it seemed to be. While the villagers feasted, a welcome breeze blew, refreshing them from the stifling heat. Later, as the women swirled and danced to the rhythm of drumbeats, the breeze gusted into wind and renewed their flagging strength. Pieces of mirrored glass stitched to the dancers' skirts and headpieces caught the sunlight and flashed as the women whirled and dipped. Faster and faster their ankle bells jingled as they stomped to the increasingly frantic beat of the drums.

Seven-year-old Sunshine, the festival's chosen child, sat mesmerized, unable to take her eyes from the dancers. No longer did she wear her tattered little-girl dress. No, on this day she was outfitted in lavish adult clothes. A beautiful new *ghaghra* enveloped her as though she were an honored bride. Carefully she smoothed the skirt, woven of red, green and white threads and splashed with bright patterns.

Like those of the dancers who whirled in front of her, Sunshine's
clothes were festooned with mirrored disks and beads. She did her
best to sit straight despite the weight of the outsized jewelry that
hung around her neck and on her thin arms.

Cautiously the little girl leaned forward to get a better view. So
much was happening—and to her! Never had people paid her so
much attention. She was just a girl, after all. That was the very reason
she had been so confounded when her great-grandmother brought
wonderful sweets for her to eat and told her that on this blessed day
she, Sunshine, would be the most honored person in the village.

When the dancing stopped, gentle hands grabbed Sunshine and
lifted her high so that everyone could see her. It was time, someone
said. The procession was about to begin.

Looking down from her exalted position, Sunshine gazed around
at her joyful neighbors. She searched among the brightly embroidered
headdresses until she caught sight of her great-grandmother looking
up at her. The old woman was laughing and cheering more loudly
than anyone. So little Sunshine laughed and cheered too, even though
the procession was carrying her toward a well-used stone table outside the village walls. Even though, at that stone table, she was to be
offered as a sacrifice to a goddess who, the villagers insisted, absolutely must be placated. Despite all this, Sunshine laughed . . . because this festival day was her blessed day.

Sunshine's *thanda* (hamlet) is a little more than 150 miles outside
India's high-tech megacity of Bangalore. But the clutch of thatched-
roof huts, closed away by a wall of stone slabs, might as well be a
village of many hundreds of years ago. For as long as any of the villagers can remember—even as far back as their oral history relates—
their practice has been to select a seven-year-old child each June, on
the feast day of the village goddess, to offer that child as a sacrifice to
their ancestors in reverence to the goddess, an innocent blood gift to
appease angry spirits. An offering to ensure that the villagers would
be safe for the coming year, that they would have food and water, that
they would stay free of disease. It must be a sacrifice worthy enough

to pacify the spirits, or the *thanda* would not be allowed to survive the year.

Hinduism mixed with animistic beliefs, then laced through with superstition. Child sacrifice. It's what the Banjara people have always done. And the Banjara are the first to insist that they do not change.

It is from the Banjara people that all the "gypsy" tribes of the world descended. Hundreds of years ago, some of their ancestors left India for central Europe. A tribal people with their own distinctive way of dressing, their own foods, their own dances and their own superstitions, the Banjara keep to themselves in villages of their own. Other Indians, who tend to look at them with disdain and distrust, willingly take the long road so they can walk around a Banjara village rather than pass through it.

Of course, little Sunshine knew nothing of all this. Nor did any of the other villagers, for that matter. Not one of them could read or write, and few had ever been outside the village. As far as they knew, everyone everywhere lived just as they did—in tiny huts with dirt floors, their goats and bulls and chickens wandering in and out as they cooked or ate or slept huddled together. And they figured that everyone everywhere sacrificed their best little ones at the June festival.

What Sunshine knew for certain was that it was most unfortunate to be born a girl. Girls were the ones who carried pots to the river to fetch water and cooked pots of millet over the kitchen fire and swept out the hut and cared for the babies while their parents worked in the fields. Even so, their families considered them a burden. Not like boys, who had the potential of bringing their parents security and possessions and good fortune.

Hope does not reach girls in the *thandas*.

Of course, Sunshine wasn't like the other girls, because her family wasn't like other families. They were Christians—the only Christians. Sunshine's grandfather was the first Banjara believer in the area. Almost fifty years earlier, when a policeman gave Sunshine's grandfather the good news of Jesus Christ, he knew he wanted to follow Christ. When he and his wife had two sons, Daniel and Joseph, they raised them to know and worship Jesus Christ, the Son of the one true God. In fact, they dedicated their boys to the Lord's work. And in an area where it was almost impossible to find someone who could read, both boys went to school, and then they went on to university and to Bible college.

None of this pleased the superstitious villagers. Because of the fear rising in them, they made dark threats against the family. "The ancestors will be angry," they insisted. "We will all pay the price." Even so, Sunshine's family stayed true to their faith.

When Daniel's wife gave birth to little Sunshine, neighbors sneered. "See, you have a girl! Just what you deserve!"

And when Daniel insisted on telling his people about God's love for them and about Jesus Christ who died to prepare a way to heaven, they said, "This Jesus, he is a Western God. How could he love Banjara people? How could he care about us?"

Still, Daniel was determined to show his people a better way. And one of the things he fought against most strongly was the horrible practice of child sacrifice. Pointing to the stone slabs that fenced off their *thanda*—each slab representing a child who had died on the stone altar—he insisted, "It is not right! God does not want us to kill our young ones! I worship the one true God, and he is a God of love. We must stop the evil practice of sacrificing our children!"

Many of Daniel's neighbors agreed with everything he said, but they were terrified of the goddess and of what she might do to them if they angered her. So they stayed in the shadows and said nothing.

In June of 1996, Daniel was called away from home to minister at another village. As soon as he was gone, his grandmother—who was not a believer—called the tribal chief and offered little Sunshine as that year's sacrifice. "To appease the goddess," she said. "To make up for all my grandson has said against her."

Daniel's grandmother took away Sunshine's tattered dress and replaced it with the beautiful new bridal dress. Then she hung huge earrings in the girl's ears, a nose ring in her nose, and draped chains of ornaments around her neck and on her arms. And all the time she cooed her loving respect to Sunshine, who had never before heard such lovely words. All day the old woman fed Sunshine delicacies the little girl had never before tasted. So Sunshine smiled with innocent trust and did everything her father's grandmother told her to do.

When words of warning finally reached Daniel, he immediately rushed for home. On the way, he met the tribal chief. "Your family is honored today," the chief informed Daniel. "Of all the children in our *thanda*, your daughter was chosen to honor our goddess."

With a gasp of horror, Daniel ran the rest of the way. When he could see the cheering procession outside the village walls, he bellowed, "Stop! You must not do this horrible thing!"

The *thanda* leaders did their best to push Daniel away, but he would not be stopped. The villagers hesitated. One by one, they looked up at little Sunshine. Then the procession jerked to a stop. Daniel reached up and grabbed his daughter, then quickly whisked her away and hid her in a remote hostel.

The village was left with no sacrifice to offer.

When the month of June ended, Daniel took Sunshine from her hiding place and moved his whole family to another city, where Sunshine would be safe. His parents did not go along, however. They decided to stay in the Banjara *thanda* with his grandmother.

Despite all that had happened, Daniel could not forget his people. Before long he began to go back to his *thanda* to work with them again. To Daniel's great joy, one young Banjara man decided that he, too, would follow Christ. Daniel invited him to be his ministry assistant. But as the two men traveled to the city together, the bus on which they were riding was hit by another bus. Daniel escaped with minor injuries, but two people were killed instantly. One was the Banjara believer.

When the villagers heard about the accident, they cried out in terror and anger, "It's your fault, Daniel! Our goddess demands a sacrifice, but you would not let us give her what was her due. Now she is taking revenge. Who will be next? Which one of us will it be?"

As panic spread throughout the *thanda,* people grew so angry at Daniel that he feared for his life. Only after many days of fasting and praying did he dare go back. His brother, Joseph, went with him, and together they did everything they could to calm the terrified villagers. "God is love," they told the people. "The goddess has no power over us. At all times, our lives are in God's hands, not hers."

Crying stopped and fear began to subside. In time, calm settled over the *thanda.*

But the very next year, Daniel's brother, Joseph, was suddenly taken ill. Within days, he died. "Look! Look! It happened again!" the villagers exclaimed. "Once more the goddess has taken her revenge!"

This time it wasn't just the villagers shouting accusations. Even those closest to Daniel were now calling him "brother killer." Once again Daniel retreated to his home in the neighboring city. He bolted the door behind him and cried out to God.

For as far back as anyone could remember, life in the *thanda* had remained unchanged. Each year in June, a child was selected for sacrifice, an innocent life to appease the spirits. It had always been so, and Banjara, as they say, do not change.

Yet Daniel refused to give up. He unbolted his door and went back out to share the good news of Jesus Christ. And the message took root in the hearts of the people. One villager after another stood in opposition to offering their children to a goddess who gripped them in bondage through terror. One after another vowed to put their future in the hands of God, who holds them in love. So many villagers, in fact, that an amazing thing happened: this Banjara *thanda* did change. They no longer practice child sacrifice.

4

Not Enough Girls

North Korea and China

*S*i-un was always sad for the people of China. Stories came to her North Korean village about the horrible conditions in that country next door. In school, the students were taught that nearly everyone in China is homeless, living in the forests or under bridges, because they do not have the benevolence of Kim Jong Il to care for them. The people in North Korea must prepare and sacrifice, Si-un was told, because at any moment the Chinese and Americans were going to march to war against them.

Even worse, in China, girls are not wanted and very few could go to school. Many Chinese baby girls are killed or left to starve after they are born. That's what Si-un was told.

All this haunted Si-un's childhood.

By the time she was a young teen, Si-un had grown used to being cold and hungry. Because of the impending war about which they were constantly warned, rations grew smaller and smaller. Now different stories made their way into her village. Two men had made the difficult arrangements to visit extended family members in China. (Why any Koreans would choose to go to that terrible place, Si-un could not imagine.) But when the men came back, they told of family farms in China run by Korean families and of fat, healthy boys and girls. The days were warm there, and people ate cabbages and chicken and fish. They had good jobs too, and lots of cars and bicycles. The men told of entire communities of North Koreans who had lived in China for a few generations and had made a good life for themselves under the watchful eye of China's central government.

Could this all be possible? Si-un wondered.

Anyone who had a relative living in China could make application to go for a few days to visit them, the men said. Of course, it would cost several months' wages, and it required lots of bribe money and many packages of cigarettes, but it was possible.

Then the men whispered of another way. An extremely dangerous way—not at all recommended, they hastened to say. Yet some had done it. Some who were starved into desperation. And if they didn't get caught, they would usually sneak back to North Korea, healthy and strong and brimming with fantastic tales about life "over there."

Were these stories of a dangerous crossing true? Si-un had to know, for she could afford no other way.

"Even if a person could swim across the river that separates our two countries without being shot by guards, there would still be danger," one uncle told Si-un. "It is very confusing without someone who speaks our language. Besides, the officers are always looking for North Koreans who do not have the proper papers to be in their country. When they catch them, they put them in shackles and bring them back to North Korea. After that, it is off to the labor colony with them."

Then, in little more than a whisper, her uncle added, "The best advice for one who would try is to seek out the people of the cross. They are always helpful and willing to share their food, even if they don't have much. They help travelers find other North Korean people."

"So, it is possible?" Si-un asked.

"Perhaps," her uncle said. "But some of what you have heard at school is not true at all. Many Chinese people are doing better now."

"Is it true what they say about girls?" Si-un asked.

"Oh, yes," said her uncle. "That I have seen with my own eyes. In China, whole villages of young Chinese men long for wives, but they stay bachelors because there are not enough girls. 'Dried branches' is what they call these men, because their family names and their family homes will not continue without wives. They are sad and angry about the situation." Then he added with a wink, "These men would love to have a beautiful and honorable girl like you, Si-un."

Si-un couldn't swim across a river. In fact, she couldn't swim at all. Yet what an intriguing thought—an adventurous journey, the chance to gain a warm home with a loving husband, to have fat children. If she married someone from her own village, her life would be miserable. The young men who liked her could not feed themselves, let alone provide for a wife and children. There simply was not enough food available. Many little ones died because they lacked proper nutrition, and those that survived were thin and sickly.

But it was impossible! Si-un did her best to put the silly idea out of her head.

Winter came, more bitter than anyone could remember. Firewood was almost impossible to find. Si-un's sickly mother could not keep warm, so she went to bed. But then she could not get up again, and before the long winter ended, she was dead. To stave off grief and despair, Si-un spent her nights fantasizing about that dangerous journey across the river and the life she might find on the other side. Of course it was just a dream, but at least in her mind she escaped far away from her loss and hunger.

Warmer weather finally arrived, but Si-un's dreams continued. She even began to talk to her father about the whispered opportunities in China. To her surprise, he did not object.

"I cannot bear to see you suffer your mother's fate," he told her. "She was too young to die."

Si-un was already in her last year of school, so she would be expected to marry soon. Right then, in her transition from girl to woman, was her time to take a big risk. Her childhood illusions were gone; she now knew North Korea was an "imprisoned nation" based on lies. If she wanted a life, if she wanted to survive, she absolutely had to get out.

Immediately Si-un began mentally packing. What would she need for such a journey? A comb, a small knife, a change of clothes, a little food—she would have to travel light. But how could she get across the river when she couldn't swim? Think as she may, she could come up with only one plan: wait for the river to freeze, then slide across it.

Si-un made her way to the river that divided North Korea from China. From the river's edge, she could look over and see people on the other side. So tantalizingly close! At sunset, people began to mill around behind bushes and small trees, and Si-un joined them. Guards kept their rifles aimed at the river. Every hour or so a shot rang out, but she never saw anyone fall.

Again and again, Si-un visited the river, each time carefully watching the guards. In time she knew exactly where each one was stationed. Exactly where the river was most narrow. Exactly where it was most shallow.

Once again winter pressed into Si-un's poor village, and once again it came with particular cruelty. Si-un watched the river grow icy. *How much longer before it is strong enough to bear the weight of a frail, frightened girl?* she wondered. She and her father talked often about her dreams of a better life. He knew of her plans, but for both their sakes, she did not tell him the details. Every day, they held each other close, knowing that their time together was short.

One day Si-un's village buzzed with the news that a young man had skated across the river. A guard saw him blur past and shot several times, but missed. Si-un was giddy with excitement. That night she went to sleep, pretending that she was that brave young man. She would wait a week or so for things to settle down, then, under the cover of darkness, she would go.

The night before her departure, Si-un sat with her father while he drank tea. She reminisced with him about her mother, and she told him she was glad to have such an honorable family. She would try to be an honorable daughter for his sake, she said, and she would always make a way to care for him. Si-un kissed her father good night, but instead of sleeping, quietly slipped into an extra set of clothes and secured her few belongings in inside pockets. Her arms and legs would have to be free.

For hours she waited, struggling to calm her pounding heart. When the night was deep, she rallied her courage and crept out of her childhood home, out beyond her fears, all the way to the river.

Si-un's departure point was well behind the trees at the river's edge. She backed up further still, then she made a running start. Diving onto her stomach, she skittered like a spider to the other side.

Not one shot was fired. Only a few voices: "Hey, did you see something? Out there on the ice? It was probably nothing."

Unable to believe her good fortune, Si-un lay still for a long time, smiling with relief. She had made it this far.

Hungry but not wanting to eat her little bit of food, Si-un looked around for edible plants. Finding none, she started to walk.

By morning, Si-un was many miles from the river. With no idea where she was going, she wandered in the direction opposite the sunrise. For two days, she continued to walk, and still she found nothing she could eat. She had just one bite left of the food she had brought with her.

Then Si-un saw the first little houses, each with a field alongside it. *Don't stop unless you see a cross,* she reminded herself. She kept walking.

On the third day, Si-un came upon a small village. Right before her eyes, a man raised a cross on top of a building. Si-un stumbled toward him.

Jumping off the ladder, the man warned in Korean, "Quiet, quiet!" He said more, but Si-un couldn't understand him. He led her inside the building and gave her water, then he hurried out.

A kind-looking woman came in with tea, a biscuit, rice and vegetables. She smiled and moaned at Si-un to show pity. It was no use trying to talk to her, because she could not understand Si-un's language, yet Si-un had the strange feeling that both the woman and the man understood the situation perfectly. Within a short time the "quiet" man returned with another, who spoke fluent Korean. Si-un cried at the sound of her own language. She told about her poor village, about her mother, about her struggle to find a good life. She also told the man the rumors she had heard about bachelor villages.

"Bachelor villages, yes," he told her, "but it is extremely dangerous for anyone to help someone like you. And we cannot promise that your life will be good once you get to a village." Then he asked Si-un, "Are you certain this is what you want to do?"

"Perhaps I could go to a Korean village inside China instead," Si-un suggested.

"Koreans are watched constantly here," her interpreter said. "I cannot put any of my friends at risk for you."

Through his Korean friend, the Chinese pastor told her of a village very much like the one about which she had heard. He would lead her there himself. They must travel many days, away from roads and paths and over mountainous land, to get deep inside a remote area where no one would be watching. They could start in a few days, as soon as she built up her strength.

Si-un had never known such abundance and such kindness. She loved the pastor's wife. How she wished she could talk to her! But there was no time to learn the language, other than a few pleasantries. The evening for departure came quickly, and the difficult journey began.

The pastor kept a fast pace, but he always had a little something for them to eat when they needed it. It was Si-un's dreams and hopes that gave her the energy to keep up with him. After four difficult days, they arrived at a village hidden deep in a forest. Both were exhausted. Men came out to greet the pastor, who seemed to know them. A few old women were there too, but no children.

No children, Si-un thought. *What a sad place.*

When the pastor explained Si-un's desire to be the honorable wife of a kind man and to have children, the men's eyes widened. *Who would want such a bold girl for a wife?* she thought. *Who would believe I would stay after such a beginning? And how would I choose a good husband from a group of strangers?*

Si-un stayed with an elderly woman while the men talked through most of the night. It was finally decided that Si-un would have to choose between two brothers who had a house and farm.

It took Si-un months to learn enough of the language to have something of a conversation. All the while she was observing her "husbands," as she called them. It became apparent that she had a tender affection for the younger brother, and he for her. But the older brother was the likely choice. So, following her best wisdom, Si-un became a sister to the younger brother and a wife to the older.

When we are established, I can send for my father, she decided.

After the first year, she gave birth to a little girl who was the delight of the village. Si-un's daughter had dozens of uncles and many grandmothers. Si-un and her family hoped for more children. But one day the hidden village—too remote for scrutiny—was visited by Chinese officials. They went house to house, demanding to see papers. Si-un could produce none. Furthermore, she spoke with a Korean accent.

The officers allowed Si-un to hug and kiss her family one last time before they tied her hands behind her back. She would be taken to a local jail and kept there overnight, then the next day she would be returned to North Korea.

As far as we know, Si-un is in prison today. Like so many in that country, she simply disappeared.

Her little girl is still in China. The child often goes to a nearby vegetable market and follows after a Korean pastor's wife, calling her "Mommy." The pastor's wife learned where the little girl lives, so now when she comes calling, "Mommy," the child is lovingly scooped up and taken back home to her daddy.

The pastor and his wife are tender people of the cross. It was they who shared the story of Si-un with us as we enjoyed a dinner together. We were joined at the large table by two men whose faces wore stunned expressions. Just the day before, they had come across the river. They never dreamed they would experience such abundance and kindness.

When injustices overlap—such as the killing of infant girls and people starved and imprisoned—the result is untold misery. Interventions must be powerful and innovative, and often they must remain hidden. Yet we do have quiet ways of helping the people of the cross who open their hearts to wanderers like Si-un.

> [Jesus said,] "I was a stranger and you invited me in. . . . Whatever you did for one of the least of these . . . , you did for me."
> (Matthew 25:35, 40)

Step Out and Take Action
for Physical Life Change

If you have been deeply affected by reading about the extreme physical needs of girls in developing countries, you can take concrete steps to intervene for them. Below is a short list of ideas, just to get you started.

- Learn one story about the physical needs of girls and tell it to others.

- Research female infanticide, nutritional disparity for girls, HIV/AIDS among females and other topics close to your heart (see the appendix for places to start).

- Consider seeking a career that addresses physical abuse of females.

- Memorize statistics about the physical abuse of girls, and share them with someone.

- E-mail the Resist the Darkness Prayer Card link, which is found at <www.resistthedarkness.org/docs/RTDBookmark.pdf>, to all your friends, family and coworkers.

- Make a video for YouTube telling how a specific story in this book has affected you.

- Pass this book along to a friend.

- Write an article for your church newsletter or a local newspaper about what you are learning in regard to the physical needs of girls.

- Comment about *Forgotten Girls* on blogs, and give updates.

- Write politicians to encourage international legislation to protect and equip female children in hard places.

Part 2

Educational Life

*W*hat does education mean to girls who live in the most desperate parts of the world?

Possibly the difference between life and death.

The "State of the World's Mothers 2005" report puts it this way: "In comparison to her educated counterparts, an unschooled girl is more likely to be poor, marry early, die in childbirth, lose a child to sickness or disease, have many births closely spaced, and have children who are chronically ill or malnourished." In all, the report lists thirty-two life-prolonging and life-enhancing benefits of educating girls.

Little wonder that in country after country, when we asked leaders to identify the greatest need of girls in their area, they answered without hesitation, "Education!"

Imagine living in a village where

An estimated 115 million children currently do not attend primary school. The majority of these are girls.

- **On average, women in South Asia have half the schooling men have.**

- **In Arab countries, 4.5 million girls do not attend school.**

- **More than 40 percent of women in Africa lack access to basic education.**

not one person can read a doctor's instructions. Where bonded laborers continue to work as virtual slaves because, unable to read the agreements presented to them, they sign away their rights with a thumbprint. Where many in the village die when fertilizer is mistaken for medicine because no one can read the warning on the label. Where no one knows that motor vehicles exist or that any building is larger than a hut. Where the laws that should protect them are useless because, uneducated and illiterate, they have no way of knowing those laws, and neither does anyone they know.

At least, not any woman.

According to a report by the World Bank, "Evidence from around the world shows that eliminating gender disparities in education is one of the most effective development actions a country can take."

An Indian leader at Oasis India, one of our partner ministries, put it this way: "An equal opportunity for an education is the only thing that will give these girls a chance."

A mother in Sudan simply begged, "Please, let my girl go to school!"

Even so, in many areas education for a girl is considered a waste of money. As a West African proverb says, "Educating a girl is like watering your neighbor's garden." But that's only one of the barriers that keep girls from school.

The children of women with five years of primary school education have a survival rate 40 percent higher than the children of women with no education.

- Girls are kept home to work.
- They are married off early—sometimes at ten or twelve, or even younger.
- Travel is often too dangerous to send girls to school.
- At school, girls are open to sexual and emotional harassment.
- The lack of toilets in schools makes modesty impossible.
- Few women teachers are available to act as models for girls.

  Yet, there is reason to hope.

5

Education for AIDS Orphans

China

or Mai Lin, hope died before she was old enough to know what it is. She was just a toddler when her mother was first afflicted with the strange sickness. Her mother grew weaker and more tired until it was difficult for her to continue going out to the fields to work. Mai Lin cannot remember the nurse who came to check on her mother. If she ever saw that nurse look suspiciously at her father slumped on the mat in the corner, then more closely examine the sores up and down his thin arms, she has no recollection of that either.

That night, as mother and daughter slept, Mai Lin's father roused himself out of his drugged sleep and stumbled out of their hut. He never came back. To Mai Lin, her father is nothing but the faintest shadow of a memory.

All around the village, people stared at Mai Lin's mother and whispered the word "AIDS," then shut their doors against her and her tiny daughter. Aunts and uncles refused to have anything to do with the desperate woman and her hungry little girl. Even Mai Lin's grandmother and grandfather turned their backs on them. Everyone was terrified that they, too, might become infected with the awful sickness.

Mai Lin's mother did everything she could to find food for her daughter and to keep her sheltered. When she was well enough, she would drag herself out to the fields to work. Because no one dared come in contact with someone suffering from AIDS, she always worked alone. When she had no other option, she resorted to begging. Occasionally, when Mai Lin wailed with hunger, her mother even stole from her neighbors. What choice did she have?

What Mai Lin *can* remember is the bitter cold of wintertime. With no coat to wear and no heavy blanket to protect her against the harsh weather, she shivered through the cold months.

Cold. Hungry. Lonely. Hopeless.

Such is the life of a child in China affected by AIDS. And there are plenty of them there. An estimated 150,000 Chinese children have lost both parents to AIDS or an AIDS-related illness, and they estimate losing an additional 250,000 over the next five years.

A drug-addicted husband brought the dreaded disease to Mai Lin's home and infected her mother. But for so many people in China—in some areas, entire villages—the cause of infection was selling blood to mobile blood banks. The banks cut costs by reusing needles and, in doing so, passed HIV from person to person to person. To pile tragedy on tragedy, the sale of contaminated blood during the 1990s received little media attention or intervention from the government. And because people had no idea they were infected, they unwittingly passed the virus along to their spouses, and mothers passed it on to their children.

Today many of those villagers infected in the original disasters are dying, oftentimes leaving children behind. They account for many of China's AIDS orphans.

As Mai Lin and her mother know only too well, HIV/AIDS in China is shrouded in stigma and cloaked in fear. This means people ignore and deny and pretend it doesn't exist. But denial only enables the scourge to multiply quicker. China now has one of the highest infection rates in the world. If the rapid spread continues unabated, it is expected that by 2010 as many as ten million Chinese will be infected.

The Chinese Ministry of Civil Affairs maintains that the definition of an AIDS orphan is a child who has lost both parents. Children who have been abandoned by mothers or fathers sick with AIDS, or those whose remaining parent is afflicted with the disease, are not to be counted. This means that children with one parent still living, even if that parent is dying from AIDS—children such as Mai Lin—cannot get the help they need.

As Mai Lin grew, her life revolved around two challenges: getting food and staying warm. Her mother had an additional preoccupation, though she never spoke of it to her daughter. She was haunted by the question "Will the time come when Mai Lin also show signs of infection?" Every cough, every fever, each illness struck terror in her mother's heart.

For a great many little girls in China, education is only a distant dream. For AIDS orphans, it is a virtual impossibility. Never in her wildest fantasies would such an idea have entered Mai Lin's mind. Yet by the time she was eight years old, and still showing no signs of the dreaded illness, her mother dared to dream about a future for Mai Lin. She had acquaintances who lived many days away, close to a school connected to a Christian ministry, and they said girls like Mai Lin were welcomed there. So though it broke her heart to say goodbye, Mai Lin's mother sent her there.

In her new home, Mai Lin's threadbare clothes were replaced with ones that really fit her and included long pants and a warm jacket that would protect her from the cold, biting wind. She was also given a blanket to wrap around her at night to keep her warm. Two times each day, she had hot food to eat—*two times!*

Very quickly Mai Lin began to grow. Her cheeks flushed pink and her eyes sparkled. For the first time in her life, she knew what it was to sleep through the night without being awakened by an aching, empty stomach.

For the first time, Mai Lin allowed herself to hope for something better in her life. To look forward to someday . . . maybe . . . just possibly . . .

For three years Mai Lin was away at school, unable to visit home. Her mother missed her daughter terribly. She could no longer go to the fields to work, yet twice each year she managed to send clothes for Mai Lin.

"I wish I could take care of my daughter," Mai Lin's mother told ministry workers in a weakened voice. "I wish I could have her with me. But look at me." She held up a twig-thin arm to show the ravages of her advancing disease.

Mai Lin was a good student. Her grades always placed her at the top of her class. But she was a quiet, shy girl, and mostly she stayed to herself. She seldom smiled. Her teacher—and the other staff members too—watched for every opportunity to praise and encourage her. They wanted to demonstrate their heartfelt affection for the lonely little girl, but they also wanted her to see Christ's love for her through them.

"I think I know what's bothering Mai Lin," one of the workers said one day. "I think she misses her mother." As the staff members shared various recollections, it became apparent that Mai Lin did indeed spend much of her time thinking about her mother, even though she had not seen her for such a long time. Immediately the workers began to make plans for Mai Lin to go back home for a visit.

But three years is a long time for a child to be apart from her mother, and much had changed for Mai Lin since she was a shivering little eight-year-old begging for food. The visit with her mother started off awkwardly. Mai Lin stared at the shriveled little woman she no longer knew. The woman looked so old and so frail. Instead of running up and embracing her, Mai Lin shrank back from the bony, outstretched arms.

The meeting was awkward for her mother too. In fact, when Mai Lin first walked in, her mother didn't believe it was really her daughter she was seeing. So tall, she was. And so strong and healthy. Could Mai Lin really have come so far in just three years?

Finally, in a soft, hesitant voice, Mai Lin's mother said, "I am so glad you came, my daughter. Every day since you left . . . every day I have longed to see you again. Just to have you with me one more time before I die. That was my greatest wish."

Mai Lin was moved by the words she heard. The workers with her could see that. Yet she didn't say a word, nor did she make a move toward her mother. The girl's hard life had taught her many lessons, and one of them was not to get attached to another person. Caring only set a person up for hurt and loss. Hadn't she lost enough already?

Even so, in spite of herself, a new light flickered in Mai Lin's eyes. She had no idea what it was, because she had never before experienced such a thing. She had no way of identifying that first glimmer of hope.

"Don't be shy," Mai Lin's teacher encouraged softly. "You may give your mother a hug if you want to."

Mai Lin hesitated. Then she stepped forward and gently put her arms around her mother. As tears filled her mother's eyes and spilled down her cheeks, Mai Lin whispered, "I miss you, my mom. I think about you all the time, and I worry that you are not well."

The reunion was short. All too soon it was time for tearful goodbyes, whispered words of love and promises to remember always and forever.

Despite the great struggle AIDS orphans face just to survive, the Chinese government discourages outside help, especially from Christians. The officials insist that there is no need for aid, that children are all well cared for.

But the villagers know better. Through words and songs and literature, they also know when the outside people who help their children
are followers of Christ. The villagers watch the kind acceptance and
the generosity, and what they see is Christ's love displayed through
those who claim his name.

Mai Lin knows she is receiving the gift of hope and a future in the
name of Jesus. We pray that one day she will also know the One in
whose name those kindnesses come to her.

6

Beautiful Music from Untouchable Girls

India

*E*very time we return home from a trip to South Asia, we hear the same comments: "India surely is booming. Those people over there must really be raking in the money."

Well, no. Certainly not the three hundred million unfortunate enough to be born at the bottom of India's caste system. Not the multitudes that, in their dire poverty, barely scrape out an existence. Not the little girl in the pinned-together blue dress.

It was in a garbage dump on the outskirts of Bangalore—India's equivalent of our Silicon Valley—that we caught sight of that smudge-faced little girl picking through piles of trash, searching for something to sell. Just as she stepped barefoot into a ditch running with raw sewage, she saw us looking at her, and she stopped. We did our best to smile. The little girl stared back, her brown eyes wide.

A rusty safety pin held the front of the girl's dress closed. Gesturing to the dress, Kay lamely offered, "That's a pretty color." The Indian teenager with us translated her words.

The child didn't move, but she never took her eyes off us.

We had just come from a school for child laborers, where we had been talking to the children and asking them questions. Nonplussed by the sight of the girl's wretched circumstances, Kay blurted out the same question she had asked child after child in the more hopeful atmosphere of the school: "What do you want to be when you grow up?"

The little girl stared.

Feeling embarrassed and foolish and overwhelmingly sad, we bid the little girl goodbye and turned to go. That's when she spoke, but in a voice so soft we almost missed her words.

"I can't be anything," she said.

For over three thousand years, this girl's people have been outcasts in Indian society. The poorest of the poor, downtrodden and oppressed. Untouchables. People less valuable than animals. According to Hindu scriptures, they are the "unborn," which is to say, it would have been better had they never existed.

Still today, members of the untouchable caste—now called the Dalits—are often forbidden to draw water from public wells. They are denied medical services and refused access to proper education. They are ordered to be Hindus even though they are barred from stepping inside a Hindu temple or reading Hindu scriptures. Should they dare convert to Christianity, their meager survival allotments are stripped away, multiplying their sufferings.

Dalits make up close to one third of India's burgeoning population, yet the vast majority live in poverty. Literacy among Dalit women is abysmally low.

For many Indian girls, the struggle for survival begins in the womb. Although it is illegal to do so, literally millions of couples use ultrasound tests to determine the sex of an unborn baby so it can be aborted should it be a girl. These expensive procedures are not available to families such as that of the little girl in the pinned-together blue dress. That is why so many girls in poverty-level families struggle into life only to be abandoned or drowned or worse.

Imagine being told from babyhood that you are a curse sent to punish your family, that you are doomed to live in misery because of some unknown evil you committed in a former life. Imagine living day after day after day with abuse and fear, knowing that as long as you live your dawn-to-late-night backbreaking workload will never end. Imagine standing barefoot in a sewer gutter, a bag of picked-over trash slung over your bony shoulder, puzzling over what a future could possibly mean. Imagine the concept of hope being too foreign to comprehend.

Less than a day's travel from that garbage dump encampment, we made our way along a path chipped into the hillside between towering pepper trees. A sweet, melodic voice beckoned to us from a makeshift church up ahead. As we stepped through the doorway, the villagers who sat packed together on the benches were singing, "Hallelujah! Hosanna!" In front, joyfully leading them in praise, was a girl with the voice of an angel.

That girl is Anne. Like the little girl in the blue dress, she belongs to the Dalit caste. But unlike that child, she does not live in a shanty in the dump. Her father, Bishop Moses Swamidas, is highly respected, one of the foremost leaders in the fight for the rights of India's Dalit people. His most effective tools are the Bible and education. So, in looking for a way to offer hope and a future to India's hungry beggar girls, we sought out the bishop's daughter.

When we told Anne what we had in mind, she said, "Only education can change the people. Dalit children do not have opportunities, because the schools cater only to high-caste people. We are underground people."

Tall and willowy, with a reserved smile and an earnest way of expressing herself, eighteen-year-old Anne is a perfect example of a young woman empowered with dignity. She has the gentle soul of an artist. Leaning forward, she talks of the joy she gets from singing and dancing and writing poetry, and of her plans to begin university.

"What would you like to be?" Kay asked her.

Anne's eyes lit up. "A professor of English literature."

And what of her beautiful voice and her unique ability to draw people together in joyful praise to God?

"I do like that," she said, flashing her shy smile. "When I was very young, I watched my father in his high position, stepping up to lead other people in praise. I think I inherited that from him. Whenever my mother and sister go to church, I go with them and sing songs for the people and teach them to sing. My whole life, I've done that. I am very thankful to God for the opportunity."

Anne's father preaches the gospel. He also preaches equality. All people—men and women, Dalit and high caste, Indian and American and African and European—all are created in the image of God. He also preaches against the social ills that plunge the poor into ever more hopeless poverty: child marriage, marriage dowries, the brutal caste system. And he preaches the vital importance of quality education, for low caste as well as high caste, for girls as well as boys.

Wherever the gospel takes root in a culture, the lives of women and girls improve. When Jesus walked the earth, he valued women as well as men—definitely not a culturally accepted approach. He still does that today.

Two states away from Anne's Kerala home, Pastor Faisal makes his way from Bangalore out to a tribal village. Three times each week, his chalkboard tucked under his arm and his pocket filled with chalk, he heads for Raakhi's house.

After Raakhi's husband died in an alcoholic haze, she struggled to survive by begging on the streets. She was the first Christian in her area, a village where not one person was able to read. When the village children see the pastor coming, they flock to Raakhi's house. They can hardly wait to hear the Bible stories they know the pastor will tell and to learn to write words on his chalkboard.

"I love these people," Pastor Faisal said. "I want to give them a voice."

And also a true hope.

Like so many tribal peoples, the religious beliefs of the villagers stretch back into ancient times before Hinduism. Worshipers of water, air and sun, they still live in terror of the unseen spirits they believe lurk everywhere, just waiting to pounce on them.

"Who can read this?" Pastor Faisal asks as he writes words on his chalkboard.

A small girl waves her hand excitedly. When the pastor smiles at her, she reads haltingly, "For God . . . so loved . . . the world . . . that he gave . . . his only Son . . ."

In another town on the other side of the state, eight-year-old Gunwanti, who lives with her family in a lean-to of twigs and rags and pieces of plastic, picks through discarded trash. As usual, she finds almost nothing salable. Little wonder, then, that when two nicely dressed young women walk across the trash dump, offering free classes, it attracts the attention of the girl's mother.

Yes, they say in answer to her question, even girls can come to the classes.

"No tuition?" Gunwanti's mother asks.

None, she is assured.

"Do I have to buy a uniform?"

No.

"School supplies?"

None. No cost for anything. The school is absolutely free.

How could Gunwanti's mother resist such a bargain?

Gunwanti could not identify letters or numbers. But then, neither could any of the other dozen or so children who came to school that first day, and who continued to come every Tuesday through Friday afternoon. Oh, how Gunwanti loved school! Not only did she begin to learn to read, but she soaked up the loving attention the teachers lavished on her. By watching them, she learned to love other people in return. She also learned to obey. These changes did not escape notice at home.

Teaching people to read and write does many things. It fights poverty by making them employable. It combats disease by enabling them to take part in their own health care. It encourages participation in the community—socially, economically and politically—and enables them to contribute to society. Not only men, but women too. Especially women. Even the most basic teaching better equips women to make informed decisions for themselves and for their families.

We told Anne about the little girl in the pinned-together blue dress, about the tribal girl at Raakhi's house and also about Gunwanti. "Really, Anne," Kay asked, "what practical difference do you think education will make for girls such as these?"

Anne's eyes glistened. "All the difference," she said. "She will read books and learn the basics of life. Every part of her life will improve. She can move out of the garbage dump. She will know her rights under Indian law, and others cannot so easily take advantage of her when she knows her rights." Then Anne added, "And she will be able to read the Bible. The Bible is the standard of life."

It was Anne who told us about Preethi.

Preethi lived on the streets of Mumbai (Bombay) with her mother and father and her blind sister. They begged or stole or did whatever else they needed to do to survive. But the day her father came back to their place on the sidewalk and found his daughters crying beside their lifeless mother was the day he gave up on the city and took the girls back to his home in South India.

There, he was lonely. He was used to having someone take care of him. So in time he found himself another wife. Though Preethi cried and pleaded, her father took her blind sister to an orphanage and left her there.

"Come, Preethi," her father said. She followed him to a one-room hut in the next village, where her sick grandfather lived. Her father sat her down in front of the closed door, then turned and walked out of her life.

After several days, the old man told his sobbing granddaughter, "This is not easy for you and it is not easy for me. But we will make it good. You are a smart girl, Preethi. You will do what no one in your family has ever done. You will go to school." So he took the girl's hand and led her down the road.

The school was the first ever to offer quality English language education to Dalits—a school for Dalits, run by Dalits. One problem though: Preethi's grandfather was poor and too ill to work, so he had no money to pay the tuition. He couldn't even afford to buy Preethi her required school uniform.

"Please take my granddaughter," he begged. "I will do anything I can."

As gently as possible, he was told there was no money to pay his granddaughter's expenses.

With tears running down his cheeks, the man clutched the little girl's hand and refused to leave. "Please, give her a chance," he pleaded. "Please! She is a very smart girl; you will see! Please, I am a Christian man myself. Please!"

The school was Bible Faith Mission Academy, headed by Bishop Moses Swamidas, Anne's father. Bishop Moses looked at the weeping grandfather, then at the young girl. Then he handed her a uniform and books. "No charge," he said.

Bishop Moses couldn't afford to pay the cost either, but he knew the value of an educated Dalit girl. So did a couple in Oregon who were searching for an organization that could help them provide education for at least one girl in India. They considered the monthly donation a bargain for a child's future.

And so, each day for the past six years, Preethi has gotten up early every morning, put on her white blouse and her burgundy skirt and matching vest, and tied her plaid necktie in place. Outfitted in her school uniform, she has walked the long trail to the academy, where she studies in English under a Dalit teacher who serves under a Dalit administration.

And in Oregon, a couple thinks of a little girl far away who is on her way to a better life and prays for her. School is far from easy, but the demanding English curriculum is preparing Preethi and her fellow students to compete for coveted university seats, something her people have never before been able to do. The difficult curriculum will also enable the children to fulfill one day what, not long ago, was an almost nonexistent breed: educated Dalits—doctors and lawyers and engineers and professors. Today, Dalits are only a tiny part of India's economic boom. Preethi and her classmates are poised to change that.

Each day Preethi enters the school under a doorway brightly painted with the school's motto: Truth, Wisdom, and Dignity.

"Jesus said, 'I am the Truth,'" Bishop Moses explained to us. "The Bible tells us, 'You shall know the truth, and the truth will set you free.' And 'the fear of the Lord is the beginning of wisdom.' When truth and wisdom combine in a person, he or she will be a person of dignity. We come from the untouchable peoples. Dignity is something we have never before known."

We followed Anne through the school doorway and stood at attention alongside the entire student body of 708 students as Preethi and two of her classmates led the opening ceremonies—in English. Public schools—the schools of the poor—teach only in local languages, dooming the Dalits to perpetual poverty and bondage.

"That must change!" Bishop Moses insisted. "The old way of education has lost its ability to empower due to the changes of globalization, privatization and computerization. Today, the need is to impart quality education based on the international standard so that students will be able to compete." Rubbing his hand across his face, he sighed and added, "Unfortunately the Dalit children, who have already been discriminated against in every walk of life, have no access to such quality education. They are too poor. Too low in society. But I am determined to see that changed."

Another amazing thing about the academy is the way it bridges the age-old chasms between castes and sexes and religions. We saw this as we made our way from classroom to classroom. A tiny girl with a red smudge on her forehead that marked her as a Hindu read aloud. Boys and girls busily wrote in notebooks. A boy worked on the computer. In Preethi's class, the boy next to her frowned over his math, then leaned over and asked Preethi for help. His light skin and narrow features told of a high-caste lineage.

In fact, of the school's current enrollment, 540 are Dalits and 180 are high caste. One out of every five is Hindu. Parents send their children because they know the school offers an excellent education. (In the center of the crowded trophy shelves stands a gold-toned shooting star on a silver-toned base, the Best School of the Year Award.)

In one classroom, two young boys sat reading, their arms around each other's shoulders. "Best friends," they said grinning. One is a Dalit Christian, the other a high-caste Hindu.

"It's sweet, but they are just children," Kay said with a touch of cynicism. "What happens when they grow up?"

Almost 95 percent of the parents come for parent-teacher meetings, Bishop Moses told us, and they all sit together and discuss what's best for their children. Together they take pride in the news that their children's school is rated at the top of all schools in their state. Together they insist on the educational standard that earned them a championship trophy for excellence in English, science, math and general knowledge. Hindus and Christians alike worked toward the school's 2006 accreditation by India's Central Board of Secondary Education in New Delhi.

"Children model the bridging of the chasms," Bishop Moses said. "They don't know what caste is, but they do know what Christianity is. They learn a new way, and their parents follow them."

As for Dalit girls, when they see their women teachers, they learn what is possible. Anne comes in and talks to them about going to the university, and they dream of going too. Never before have many of them seen an educated woman. But they go home and they read to their parents. These children will be better citizens of the Dalit communities of tomorrow. And the future church in India will have powerful new leaders because of them.

"Dalits are poor all over India, and it is difficult to pay for school here," Anne told us. "Many mothers are suffering now to get an education for their children that will mean a different life for them tomorrow."

Even though the children see their parents' pride, they cannot yet understand what their parents know: because of what these young ones are accomplishing, the next generation will have a chance at opportunity, equality and hope.

"What would you like to be when you grow up?" Kay asked Preethi.

"A writer," she said, "because I want to be a voice for my people."

Never would Preethi's mother have dared to dream such a dream! But Preethi does, because she looks at Anne and she sees that it is possible.

Perhaps one day Preethi's own daughter will have trouble believing there was a time when girls had to be satisfied simply to wish and dream.

7

Given by the Chief

Senegal

The African sky glowed orange over the village of Mbana. A momentous night awaited the villagers, the most exciting in anyone's memory. Chief Jawara had called for the celebration in honor of his only son's homecoming. As drums pounded, 1,400 people who lived outside the village also poured in to enjoy the festivities, all eager to take part in the feasting, dancing and ceremony. They were not disappointed.

As part of the celebration, this night two girls would be given away by the chief. We looked at the chosen ones—ten-year-old Esmee and her little sister, Afia, who was barely nine—and wondered what "given away" meant.

Clapping women lined up on one side of the fire, where they shuffled and chanted an energetic song about village life for hardworking mothers. The men sat in small groups and watched.

Suddenly one man jumped up. Waving his arms, he danced toward a different group of men, who were busy chewing roasted goat meat. He tore off his shirt and threw it on the ground in front of them. The circle of men looked at each other to see who would be brave enough to dance. When one of them jumped up, the first dancer sat down. The dance continued this way until every group had its chance to perform. Everyone laughed and clapped as each man tore off his shirt and threw it down, as each man danced more outrageously than the one before.

When the dancing finally stopped, the chief stood up in front of the roaring fire. He grasped his walking stick and, with a wizened arm, raised it high over his head. Every drum stopped. Every mouth shut. No one wanted to miss the words of their leader, the host of the great feast.

"One day my son was with us out in the field, and then he walked away and disappeared into the desert," the chief began. "I did not know where he was. Day after day I looked for him and wondered what had happened to him. Was he hurt? Had he been eaten by an animal? Did someone take him as a slave?" The chief choked with emotion. "Where was my son!"

We already knew the story—as did almost everyone else—but the pageantry of the evening kept us breathless. In Senegal, storytelling is true art.

The chief said that for three full years he and his wives didn't know whether their son was dead or alive. They were heartbroken. The only thing that kept the chief alive through those sad days was his love for the village. It was desperately poor, and since he had been entrusted with its leadership, he was determined to do the best he could for the people in spite of his misery. Many nights he went to sleep with Mbana's troubles stirring in his head. It was the only thing that could press back his grief and worry over his son.

"I wished I could do more so the women would not have to walk into the desert and carry heavy loads of water," the chief said. "I wished their children did not drink water that made them sick and gave them brown, broken teeth. Other villages have deep, clean wells. Other villages have small schools for their children. We should have those things in Mbana too, I thought. But we did not even have rain for our crops. What must we do to get the spirits' help so that the people would not suffer so? That was what stirred in my mind during those troubled times."

The chief's talk of the spirit world didn't surprise us. In West Africa, questions about appealing to spirits came up frequently. From time to time a traveling Muslim teacher called, a marabout, would come to the village and tell the chief all the things God demanded of the people in order to gain his favor. Much of it had to do with filling the pockets of the marabout. When people had problems, they didn't turn to him. They asked the shaman for help.

It was said that the shaman—or witch doctor—could bid the spirits to do special things for those he favored or bring harm to those who displeased him. Because of his power, the shaman was greatly feared in the village. And because his help came at a high price, he was one of the wealthiest men in the area. Often the chief sat with the shaman and sought his wisdom about ways to get help for the people of the village. Even so, nothing good ever seemed to happen.

As the fire crackled behind him, Chief Jawara continued with his story: One night, two young village men, Lucien and Ames, came to see him. They had just listened to a spiritual teacher who regularly came to Mbana, and the teacher's words made them curious about many things. So they asked the chief, "If marabouts are good teachers, why do they take children and turn them into slaves and beggars?"

We thought this was a pretty good question. Impoverished parents often gave their boys to a marabout in the hope that the children would learn his teachings and grow up to become spiritual teachers themselves. But everyone could see that the "given boys" are little more than slaves, exploited as dirty, hungry beggar children, often beaten if they failed to collect enough money for their marabout.

The chief told the people that Lucien and Ames explained to him that when the spiritual teacher spoke of great teachers of the past, he mentioned a prophet named Jesus. "They told me that this Jesus sounded wise, helpful and kind to everyone. They said maybe they should find out more about him and seek his help for our village."

The chief told the people that he, too, had heard talk of Jesus. People in one particular village knew much about this prophet, and when men came through Mbana from that village, they sat with the chief and talked to him about Jesus and his powers. So, Chief Jawara said, Lucien and Ames walked all day through the desert to that other village. When they finally arrived in the evening, everyone was gathered together, watching pictures that moved and talked. Such a thing! The pictures were all about Jesus.

"Lucien and Ames discovered that this prophet loved every person and everything, and that he had created them all," Chief Jawara told the people. "The pictures told them that Jesus is God who came to earth as a man so he could make payment for sin. He is now Lord over everything, and he sees and intervenes on the earth. The pictures told that Jesus taught people to bless children and take care of them. All this sounded so wonderful to Lucien and Ames that they decided right then that they would follow the words of Jesus. Their new village friends told them to come back to their village and show respect to me, their chief, and tell me all that they had learned."

Chief Jawara paused in his story long enough for the people to fully grasp the importance of his words. When everyone seemed fully impressed, he reached dramatically over the fire and continued: "I listened to all that Lucien and Ames spoke. Then, for the first time in three years, I began to hope that someone could help me find my son. I asked them if they would talk to Jesus and see if he would tell them where my son was. They did that right in front of me. To our astonishment, as soon as they prayed to Jesus, my son appeared."

At this, the entire village gasped.

The chief looked over at his son, who was just then helping himself to the most delicious and prized part of the goat—the intestines swollen with half-digested vegetables and millet. In offering it to him, the father had demonstrated to the entire gathering that this son was the favored one, the honored guest. As all eyes turned to him, the son shrugged and smiled, then scooped up another mouthful.

The chief explained that, like so many teenage boys, his son had decided his small village was boring. And because it was so poor, without even a school, it held no future for him. So one day he simply walked away, headed for a big town where he could make a better life for himself. But that's not what happened, the chief said. The boy's three years away were a terrible disappointment. No one wanted to help yet another in a flood of hungry young men. He spent some time with a marabout, but that didn't last long; he had no desire to live as a slave. To survive, he was forced to do things he never imagined himself doing. Then, one day, overwhelmed by loneliness for his simple village home, he got up and made his way back to Mbana.

"My son who was lost is found!" the chief exclaimed. The excited crowd broke into wild cheers.

"So, from this night forward, I give everyone in Mbana permission to listen to Lucien and Ames. They will tell you good things about God for you and for your children. They will tell you about Jesus. To prove how much I believe the truth of what they say, I will give two children to this new way."

Chief Jawara pointed his walking stick into the crowd, and the two little girls were led up to stand with him in front of the fire. They were clearly terrified. Surely they had heard rumors of what happens when girls are "given." They become slaves, like the boys given to the marabouts, but much worse. Esmee and Afia gulped back tears.

We looked at each other. Where was this going? Was there anything we should do? Or could do?

"If Jesus loves these children, he will answer your prayers for them," the chief proclaimed. "They will grow strong and healthy. They will go to school. We will see what Jesus does for them."

"Wait! Wait!" we wanted to cry. "This isn't right. No one should give away little girls!"

When we were finally able to get a private word with Lucien, everyone on our small team expressed concern about the girls being given away—even to someplace as nice as a church. Where would they be taken? What would happen to them?

"They will continue to live with their parents, just like before," Lucien assured us. "The difference is that now it will be the responsibility of the church leaders to take care of the girls' needs the way Jesus would take care of them. Their education, their health, all their needs belong to our church. And the entire village will be watching."

"It's a great opportunity to see Christ's love in action," Michele said.

"Yes," Lucien replied. "The difficulty is that Ames and I are the only two in the church."

"Maybe we can help," Michele said.

Back home in the United States, we got to work sharing the story of Esmee and Afia. We told about the challenge given by Mbana's chief and of Lucien and Ames's determined acceptance of that challenge. We invited people to "adopt" the village and work alongside our brothers in Christ as they raised the girls in Jesus' name. Drawing on the crosscultural partnership expertise of Dr. Daniel Rickett and his team of project managers, we would see that funds were used wisely by partnering with a local African ministry, Mission Inter Senegal (MIS). We promised to continue to visit the village regularly and to report back on the progress.

Today, Esmee and Afia are fourteen and thirteen years old. They are progressing well in the new school built in the village, and they want to go on and get more education. "So we can succeed," Esmee told us.

If the girls lived in another village, they would already be married. Maybe they would be maimed for life by a horrid but common complication of having babies at too young an age: tearing that causes a permanent opening called a fistula, awful leakage and terrible suffering and shame. It could even be that they would have died in childbirth like so many girls who have not finished growing when their babies come.

The entire village is prospering. Today Mbana has a deep community well with seven fountains that pipe clean water throughout the area. Families can pay a few extra coins to the community for rights to use the fountain to water their gardens. For the first time, Mbana grows a great variety of vegetables, more than the village needs, and family farms sell produce to other villages. The village also has a grinding mill, which means that the women no longer have to spend hours in the desert sun pounding millet. Now young mothers have time to attend health and hygiene classes, so more babies and children are surviving. And since women from other villages also come and grind their millet, the mill is a source of income for the village.

The church has grown as well. Lucien and Ames are still there, and more than two hundred families have joined them. It is a vibrant church, eager to reach out to surrounding villages and share the hope of Jesus' love. They saw that love displayed by Christians around the world as they worked together to raise two young girls as Jesus would do.

Chief Jawara is now a Jesus follower. And the powerful and feared shaman is no longer selling villagers the power and fear of evil spirits. Now he tells them the gospel story, for he, too, is a follower of Jesus.

Two village girls. Two windows of hope and blessing in a dark area.

8

A New Way

Egypt

$\mathscr{A}$ gentle touch on Kay's arm, then a soft voice barely discernible over the noise of some fifty teenagers laughing and talking: "Can I talk to you?" A teenage girl in blue jeans and a crisp red shirt stood before us.

"It's about my . . . my cousin," Anissa said hesitantly. "Her father . . . he, uh, he does things he shouldn't do to her. Sexual things. All the time, ever since she was little. My cousin, well, she doesn't know what to do."

We had come to Cairo because of our interest in a program begun by a Christian Egyptian physician who recognized a dire need to teach boys to respect girls, and girls to respect themselves. None of these teenagers had ever seen us before. Yet Anissa's approach didn't come as a total shock. The program leader had told us, "Don't be surprised if some girls confide in you. Many find it easier to talk to a foreigner than to their own leaders. Everyone has secrets, and they worry that a local person might talk." Or might look askance and ask, "Are you sure it's your *cousin*? And just which cousin might that be?"

"How fortunate your cousin is to have you," Kay said. "That can be a hard subject to discuss." Anissa's face wrinkled up and tears began to flow.

Family honor. Silence. In a society where abuse of girls and women is tolerated, if a man is abusing a girl, it is automatically assumed she is the one at fault. Surely she did something to tempt him, people think. So the abuse is silently tolerated.

According to experts, abuse of all kinds against women is extremely common in the Middle East. Recent studies show that fully one-third of Egyptian women are assaulted by an "intimate partner." The majority of these women never tell anyone—certainly not the police. Only 44 percent say they have even told a family member.

"But now my . . . my cousin's brother . . . he started doing it too!" Anissa wept. "Sometimes she wants to die."

Like father, like son. One generation learns from the generation before it.

By watching their fathers and grandfathers and uncles, boys learn it is permissible to treat the women of the family in such ways. Everyone seems fine with it; that's just what men do. If a father shows no respect for his wife and daughters, his son can hardly be expected to act any differently toward the women and girls around him.

"Has your cousin told her mother what's happening?" we asked.

"Oh, no," Anissa said. "She is too afraid to say anything to anyone."

How many times might even Anissa have longed to touch her mother's arm and, in a voice barely above a whisper, to beg, "Can I talk to you? It's about my friend. My cousin. *Me.*"

The 44 percent of girls and women who do speak of abuse most often tell a family member, according to the survey. Yet their families are the very ones most likely to condone what is happening to them— or at least to brush it aside. So, if Anissa had gone to her mother, how would her mother have reacted? Probably the same way her own mother reacted a generation before. Probably by pretending it wasn't happening, or at least that she hadn't heard about it.

Like mother, like daughter. Generation following generation.

"Has your cousin ever told her father to stop?" Kay asked Anissa. "Or did she ever say no to her brother?"

Anissa shook her head. "She never says anything. That's not how they do things in our family." Don't speak your mind. Keep your feelings to yourself. As for opinions, you shouldn't even have them.

It is precisely because so few girls and women feel free to speak up that antiabuse programs, such as Smart Heart, are vital.

Right now, many organizations are making a variety of health and education options available to poverty-level women throughout Africa and the Middle East, as well as across Asia and Latin America. And in many cases, the results are excellent. A good number of these programs accomplish much by improving the status of poor women and opening up to them a range of possibilities for starting businesses and earning an income. Nor do the programs benefit the women alone. Entire families and whole communities are changed by the opportunities they bring. For instance, when women are able to work and bring an income into the family, their daughters reap myriad benefits, such as an improved diet with more protein, better health care options and access to education.

Yet all of this does not automatically bring about cultural change. Traditional attitudes are deeply entrenched, and it takes time, effort and specific action to change them. If such concepts as the right to be free from oppression and abuse, the right to speak freely in one's family and the right to share opinions are to prevail, they need to begin in those who are young.

According to the survey quoted earlier, over 85 percent of the women who responded stated that they believe beatings are justified for wives who misbehave. And what constitutes punishable misbehavior? Such things as talking back to their husbands, the women said, or burning food or wasting money.

In a culture where women must stay in their place and silently bear whatever is done to them, where denial and silence are esteemed values for a female, where a woman submits to a beating for scorching the rice, where a mother must turn her back on an abused child for fear of the consequences—in such a culture, real change requires much more than financial programs for women and girls. It requires an altered mindset for an entire culture.

And that's not at all easy to accomplish.

When we first arrived in Egypt, before the Smart Heart meeting in Cairo, we spent time in the picturesque expanse of the small farming villages of Upper Egypt, a land of sugar-cane fields and lush vineyards that reaches far south along the banks of the Nile River. In that slower-moving, more conservative area, men wear traditional long robes and travel the rutted roads on overloaded donkey carts. It's quite a contrast to smog-clogged Cairo, a city of twenty million people. In Upper Egypt we saw some of the country's poorest communities and also its most Christian.

In the meeting room there, a small circle of girls shared their experiences. They punctuated their words with smiles and friendly gestures, asking each other questions, listening to the answers and sharing opinions—sometimes with tears and occasionally with sparks of anger. A skinny thirteen-year-old in a pink, ruffle-necked T-shirt sat on one side of us, and on the other side were two sisters in jeans and twin pink sweaters.

Lots of pink. It was hard not to think back to grade school and the chant: "Pink, pink, you stink like a girly-girl." And hard not to remember that softball-game taunt "You throw like a *girl*."

One girl stopped in mid-sentence and looked around her. "Will Zahra ever come back?" she asked.

The girls explained to us that Zahra used to come to their group. When she stopped coming, the group leader went to her house and found out that her father had arranged a marriage for her within the month.

The girl in the pink ruffles interrupted. "It wasn't even legal! The legal age for marriage is eighteen, and she is only fifteen."

"Zahra wanted to be a teacher," said another girl. "That's what she told us. She didn't want to quit school."

We asked what happened next. "She told her father she wouldn't get married," the girls replied.

Zahra's father was amazed at his daughter's refusal. It never occurred to him to ask her opinion in the matter. But since it obviously meant so much to her, he went to the boy's father and told him the wedding was off. That man was not nearly as understanding, however. He flew into a rage and yelled, "You dishonor my entire family!" Then he threatened, "I will kill your daughter, then the dishonor will be yours."

Zahra's father could bear many things, but he was a proud man. He could not bear to be dishonored. In a hushed voice, the first girl said, "Zahra's father told the man, 'She is my daughter, so I will do it myself. I will kill her.'"

"When we heard about it, I went to see Zahra's father," the group leader said. "I begged him to reconsider, but he would not. How could he, he said, when it was a question of his honor?"

We asked what happened. "She is married," the girl in ruffles told us.

"But at least she tried," added another girl. "That's something."

In Cairo, the small group of fourteen- and fifteen-year-old girls was much more sophisticated than the clutch of thirteen- to nineteen-year-olds in Upper Egypt. The discussion groups followed a large coed group time. And the Cairo girls chatted on their cell phones and sent each other text messages as they waited to begin. Even so, their issues were much the same as those of the small-town girls: guilt, inferiority, longing for love, tales of abuse.

"Safia," the leader said to a twig-thin girl with wiry curls, "would you be willing to share your story with our guests?"

Safia nodded and took a deep breath. "I was almost fourteen when my father told me I was to be married," she said. "I told him, 'No, I will not agree to that.'"

Her father had stormed and threatened, but she remained firm. "I will go to the authorities if I must," she said. "The law says I do not have to marry so young." Her father told her that since she chose to dishonor him, she would have to leave his house forever. "He banished me from my family," she said. In a culture where family is everything, such a threat could be a death sentence.

"I would not marry," Safia said. "I was frightened and sad, but I had learned to set my boundaries. I kissed my mother goodbye, and I hugged my sister and my brother. Then I went to my friend's house and knocked on her door."

After many days, a message came for Safia at her friend's house. It was from her brother. He too had taken the course on relationships and communication, and the situation in their family was not tolerable to him.

"He said that my mother missed me," Safia said. "He said I could visit her if I wanted to, that he had talked to my father and I would be safe."

So Safia went to visit her mother, who asked her to stay and eat dinner with the family. Safia did, and her father did not object. Her brother said that since it was so late, it would be good for her to spend the night. Her father said nothing, so Safia spent the night.

"And I stayed home," Safia said. "I continued in school, and my father never mentioned the marriage. My father does not feel dishonored, because he never personally gave in to me. It was my brother and my mother who gave in and made the apologies."

We looked around the group and wondered what all these girls' lives would be like when they had teenage children of their own. We wondered about Anissa too.

So far, ten thousand girls and boys have gone through this program. The goal is to reach fifteen thousand more each year. If we come back in ten years, will we see an appreciable change in Egypt? No. If we come back in fifty years? Maybe.

Step Out and Take Action
for Educational Life Change

You probably feel as we do: after physical health, few things are more empowering to girls than literacy and education. If education is the issue most pressing on your heart, take steps below for bold action to help educate destitute girls.

- Create a piece of art showing how education empowers girls.

- Text a fact you have just learned to a friend. Ask that person to pass it on.

- Write a letter to your legislators, asking them to support investment in education for girls in developing countries.

- Post <www.SistersInService.org> as a website and interest on your Facebook profile, and share it with your networks.

- Add Sisters In Service as a charity for your sorority or other group. Host an informational program to kick off the new partnership.

- Download a picture of one of the girls in this book to use as your screensaver. You can find them at <www.resistthedarkness.org/docs/Forgotten_Girls_Photo_Gallery.pptx>.

- Contact local media to encourage an article on the educational needs of girls.

- Make your own video about what the lack of education for girls means to the next generation and our world, and post it on YouTube.

- Mobilize junior-high girls or Girl Scout troops on behalf of girls who cannot afford to go to school. Girls in the United States can make bead bracelets, sell them, then donate the money to provide education for other girls.

- Host a small dinner party with the parents of children in private schools and show the Resist the Darkness PowerPoint presentation to raise awareness and educational funds. This can be accessed at <www.resistthedarkness.org/truth.shtml>.

- Pray for families to invest in the education of their daughters as well as their sons.

- Ask your book club to sponsor a book sale to provide for dozens of HIV/AIDS orphans like Mai Lin who live with impoverished relatives.

PART 3

Sexual Protection for Life

A five-year-old shouldn't have to run away from home and hide in a tree for safety. Girls shouldn't be married because they are tricked or bought. And no girl should ever, ever be sold to a brothel—not by anyone, but especially not by her parents.

Yet one of the horrors of our time is that what should never happen is happening every day. In place after place after place. To girl after girl after girl.

More than one million children and babies are trafficked every year, and the number is increasing.

The fact is that many girls in developing countries are routinely subjected to sexual abuse. Violence often begins before birth and continues throughout life:

- prenatally: coerced pregnancy, rape during war

- infancy: physical abuse, lack of medical care

- childhood: incest, sexual abuse, child prostitution
- adolescence: sexual harassment, rape, forced prostitution, forced marriage
- adulthood: marital rape, sexual harassment, murder

This is not an exhaustive list, to be sure, but it is long enough to chill us in our tracks.

Sex trafficking of girls is rampant, especially in Eastern Europe and Asia, and that's the form of sexual exploitation with which we are most familiar. But it isn't the only form this injustice takes. In India, Nepal and Bangladesh, for instance, many girls are forced into marriage. In Central Asia, girls are kidnapped and forced to be brides.

In most countries forced marriage is against the law. The problem is that the laws are both inadequate and weakly enforced. Also, money is terribly enticing to so many people who stagger under oppressive poverty.

Sex traffickers in particular are well funded, well organized and constantly on the lookout for the most vulnerable girls. When they spot a likely target, they move in with ruthless, creative ploys designed to win the victim's confidence, then to trick and coerce her. They promise marriage, a job, the opportunity to go to school—anything and everything.

But the reality can be deadly. In 2001 alone, an estimated twelve thousand girls were trafficked from Nepal to the brothels of India. It is believed that a quarter of a million Nepali girls are in India's teeming brothels. Two-thirds of them are HIV-positive. Few will live to see their twenty-fifth birthday.

> "Poverty coupled with illiteracy provides a breeding ground for human traffickers."
>
> THE RISING NEPAL, 2007

Victims should not have to pay the devastating price for this awful form of slavery. Yet girls are routinely threatened, raped, abused physically and emotionally, and sometimes even killed by sex traffickers. The strangle grip of human trafficking reaches beyond individual victims and even past the most egregious nations. It also occurs with staggering frequency in the United States, Canada and Great Britain. The U.S. State Department says trafficking undermines the health, safety and security of every nation of the world.

The market is over there—and it is right here. It includes Western Europeans and Americans, and the hunger for pornography is so often fueled and fed by the little girls bought and sold by traffickers. One much-publicized child-porn industry in Sri Lanka is said to involve thirty thousand children.

The problem is everywhere.

9

Temporary Wives in Timbuktu

Mali

*W*alking along short, sandy alleyways in Timbuktu, we turned corner after corner under fierce heat and gusts of whirling sand. We strained to take in thousands of years of history as our Malian friends pointed out ancient buildings that showed influences of the Moors, the Europeans, adventurers and missionaries.

Timbuktu, Mali, on the edge of the Sahara Desert, has often featured prominently in legend for being nearly impossible to reach and also for having gold buried in its sand dunes. Neither is true, of course. What has been consistently true over the centuries is the suffering that falls on the most vulnerable in this drought-ridden region.

Many of the proud, nomadic camel herders we encountered have lost all their livestock to the persistent drought. They walk the town like great barons, yet they own almost nothing. Around every corner we saw squatters' dome-shaped tents, fashioned out of reed mats stitched together to create a little shade. And languishing everywhere were sand-covered young women and nearly naked boys and girls.

One particularly tall man with a long beard, wearing a white robe and blue turban, seemed to be everywhere. He walked alongside a little girl whom we guessed to be about ten years old. The man definitely seemed to be going, well, from place to place. We would round one corner, and he was there. We would round another corner, and there he and the girl were again. Later, as we talked with our African friend, Grace, we learned the likely fate of that little girl.

Grace, a stately and passionate local woman, is the leader of the Women's Training Center in Timbuktu. She lovingly reaches out to girls like the one we kept seeing. The tall man, Grace told us, is a "religious leader." Most likely he was making "arrangements."

"The girl is probably a young virgin, being sold by her parents," Grace told us. "A contract will be written up, perhaps even a ceremony performed. But almost certainly she will be divorced in a short while. And if she should become pregnant, she must bear the responsibility alone."

Shocked, we asked if this was happening to other girls as well. "Oh, yes!" Grace said. "Timbuktu is filled with hungry street children who came from such temporary marriages."

The government is at long last recognizing the serious social threats that result from this practice, including the HIV/AIDS epidemic raging through West Africa, Grace told us.

"These girls are just children. They should be playing and learning. Instead they are used as long-term prostitutes. They have no say in their future." Then, with great tenderness and deep emotion, Grace added, "God has a plan for these girls, and yet people exploit their vulnerabilities in temporary marriages."

"We are shamed by our lives."

A "TEMPORARY WIFE" IN TIMBUKTU

Grace went on to explain that there are three types of temporary marriage that allow men the sexual release they crave without them technically committing the sin of adultery: work marriage, hidden marriage and tiny hut marriage.

In a *work marriage,* an Arab man from a

country such as Libya or Morocco comes to Timbuktu for work and sees a girl he desires. Because he is wealthy and her family is impoverished, and because he is a man and she is only a girl, he negotiates a large dowry with her parents—often as high as one million francs or more (over three thousand U.S. dollars). Rather than protest, the girl's parents are honored that a wealthy man would choose their daughter. Religious contracts are signed, and within a day, a festive marriage ceremony is put together on the outskirts of town.

Everyone in our group had questions about how long such a marriage would last.

"That depends on the husband," Grace told us. "It might be two weeks, two months, two years—whatever he wants. Generally it lasts only until his business dealings in Timbuktu come to an end."

In a *hidden marriage*, or *Sere Heji*, a man already has a wife or even two wives—women of high social standing. Those wives will not tolerate an additional wife of low status. So the man simply chooses to keep the unacceptable girl hidden where he can "visit" her from time to time. Once the other wives find out about her, the marriage ends.

Our next question: "Why would a girl agree to such a marriage?"

"Money," Grace says. "The dowry her family receives is far greater than they could ever hope to get from a traditional marriage."

A man who wants to initiate a hidden marriage may send the equivalent of one thousand U.S. dollars to the girl's family for several nights in a row, along with clothes, shoes and perfume. Finally he arrives with a religious official who will complete the marriage ceremony by reciting the *Fatila* (opening prayer) and pronouncing the two "husband and wife." Because the parents have previously been notified that their daughter is wanted by high nobility, such a marriage can be expected to increase the bride's family's social status, not to mention their economic level. As for the new wife, she and her descendants will receive whatever the husband chooses to give them.

When asked how long this hidden marriage would last, Grace said: "As long as the girl remains 'in good spirit, good behavior and in submission,' or until his other wife finds out about her."

A *tiny hut marriage* (*Sneha*) is specifically intended for a man who is overtaken by sexual desire while he is traveling. He wants to avoid adultery, since that is so great a sin, so he simply asks to talk to the parents of any unmarried girl in the area, and he offers them a gener-ous dowry in exchange for one or several nights with their daughter. The "marriage" will end at daybreak of the day he leaves. Though the bond was sealed by a religious proclamation, all he has to do is pro-claim, "I divorce you, I divorce you, I divorce you," and the marriage is over. The man goes home "guilt free." The parents count their new-found wealth. The girl's life is destroyed.

Halima's parents married her to a stranger, and he divorced her six days later. But even after he divorced her, he continued to visit from time to time and to bring food. Halima's one hope was that he would continue to care for her.

"I felt such shame because I was no longer a virgin," Halima told us. "Who would want to marry a girl like that?"

So deep is the disgrace after the marriage is over that some girls go right on selling themselves—much more cheaply, of course, since they are already used.

But for Halima, even bigger problems lay ahead. She was pregnant. Still a young teen when she gave birth to her baby boy, she suffered terribly with internal and external injuries and scarring. "The doc-tors told me I could not have any more children," she told us. "And I suffer such pain that sometimes I want to die. But I have to stay alive for my baby. I am the only person who cares for him."

"What about your baby's father?" Michele asked. "Did he help you?"

"When he found out I could have no more children, he stopped com-ing to see us," Halima said. "He also stopped making sure we had food."

At the height of her desperation, Halima learned from other girls that she could get food free at the Women's Center. People at this simple, cinder-block structure—an unexpectedly valuable place for someone like Halima—would also provide her with training so that she could support herself and her son. "That's why I came," she said.

While Halima is in class, her son joins the many other children who pour into the new Noah's Ark Day Center, built and funded by friends in the United States. Loving Malian teachers teach the children basic reading, writing and math. The little ones receive a meal, and they can nap in a relatively cool building.

When Halima graduates with her class of one hundred women, she expects to have a tailoring skill and a sewing machine. The waiting list of young mothers is long, but each candidate is carefully considered, and the program is expanding as money is available.

One thing we specifically wondered was whether or not Halima was learning about the love of God. And so Michele gently inquired about this.

"The teacher is very good to me," Halima said. "I like to learn. But I stopped praying to God a long time ago because of the hardness of my life. I have lost hope. Maybe someday my hope will come back to me."

And it is so for Salimata, one of the older women at the center. She, too, knows all about being weary and destitute. But, with hope radiating from her sun-leathered face, she told us, "I came here with such sadness and shame, but I found out that God loves me. I do my best to encourage the younger women until they too come to know God's love."

Then Salimata said something else: "These girls have been let down by so many people. They must not be let down here too." At times women came to the end of their year of learning and practice only to find at their graduation that no sewing machine was available for them, Salimata explained. The center was set up to provide the training, not the expensive tools of the trade. Sewing machines were a bonus when the center could afford them.

"That cannot be!" Michele said. And right then she made a commitment: "We will do all we can to see that every single woman who works hard to learn will graduate with the tools she needs to build her new life."

A group of businesswomen in the United States who love to teach sewing have joined us to see that commitment become a reality. Their business, Front Door Fabrics, gives a percentage of its sales for sewing machines and lessons in Timbuktu, and they ask for donations at the checkout counter as well.

What an opportunity to raise awareness of the plight of temporary wives by helping those who are rising above the abuse and exploitation!

10

Kidnapped!

Kyrgyzstan

The tiny Central Asian country of Kyrgyzstan boasts gorgeous glaciers, pristine lakes and snowcapped mountains. But the realities for the Kyrgyz people are harsh indeed. Ninety-four percent of the terrain is mountainous and unfruitful. Over half the people (55 percent) live below the poverty line, and the average income is 280 U.S. dollars per year. Alongside towns are clusters of yurts—tent homes of nomadic herders with a design that has been unchanged for thousands of years.

In ancient times Kyrgyz men on horseback would ride through a field and snatch unsuspecting girls to forcibly wed. Some things have changed since ancient times. Much has not.

On most any day, somewhere in Kyrgyzstan or a neighboring country, a vehicle bulging with young men pulls alongside a school girl. She is grabbed and pulled into the vehicle, then whisked to someone's house. There the girl is physically restrained by four or five women from the abductor's family, who take turns offering soothing words and, if the girl does not stop fighting, violent threats. She is forcefully dressed in traditional bridal garb. When she is too weary to fight off the wedding veil, it signals her resignation to the "marriage." Guests and a feast are ready and waiting. No matter how the girl protests, the marriage will be consummated and her forced labors will begin.

Some girls die during the kidnapping and marriage, either accidentally at the hands of their captors or by suicide, when the shame of rape is simply too great to bear.

In Kyrgyzstan, nearly one third of all marriages are the result of "bride-stealing." Since 1991, when the country became independent from Russia, the violent practice has been on the rise despite new laws that prohibit arranged kidnapping and child marriage. Offenders are never prosecuted, and families feel no sense of shame for committing the kidnappings and rape. In fact, they celebrate it.

According to the British Broadcasting Company, Kyrgyzstan is not alone. Bride-napping or stealing also occurs in neighboring Turkmenistan, the Caucasus and Turkey—and even in Japan and Ethiopia.

Why such a violent practice? Many shrug and blame the high cost of traditional marriage. Elaborate weddings and the bride price for desirable girls can run as high as one thousand U.S. dollars. And, really, they say, a girl is only family property, and valuable assets do get stolen. Besides poor, uneducated girls expect it, really. That's what they say.

Meerim, a graduate of the local university, had a good job as office manager at an Internet café. A modern, progressive young woman, she liked blue jeans, wore her hair in a stylish cut and surfed the Internet. She was unique in another way too: she was a follower of Jesus Christ.

As recently as fifteen years ago, the entire Christian church in Kyrgyz was made up of twenty believers, but by 2000 it had grown to 3,500. Meerim was part of this growth. Her mother insisted that such a wonderful, desirable young woman as she absolutely must marry early, but Meerim refused. She had other plans. Better plans.

During a holiday break, Meerim arranged to visit a girlfriend in Bishkek, Kyrgyzstan's capital. As she waited outside a café, Rahat, a young man she knew only casually, stopped to chat. Meerim mentioned how excited she was to have the chance to get together with friends for the holiday. But she was waiting for her girlfriend to get off work, she told him, and it would still be a while.

"Won't you come inside the café and have tea with me while you wait?" Rahat suggested.

He seemed like a nice enough guy. And they would be in a public café, within sight of the street. What could happen there? Besides, Meerim wasn't really thinking about Rahat. Her mind was on the relaxing holiday ahead.

As Meerim sat with Rahat over tea, her conversation was light and simple, just a friendly chat. When it came time for her to meet her friend, Meerim excused herself to go outside and catch a bus.

"Oh, please, do allow me to drive you to meet your friend," Rahat offered.

It is a nice offer, Meerim thought. *Buses are such a nuisance.*

As they drove along, Rahat mentioned that he needed to stop by his home for a minute to pick something up. But Rahat's parents, extended family and friends were all in the house waiting for them. Fresh-baked, traditional Kyrgyz wedding bread was piled on the table and an entire wedding feast had been laid out. Panic arose in Meerim, but before she could react, women grabbed her and forced her into the house. Rahat's mother stepped forward, carrying the traditional bride's white headscarf.

Meerim's screamed out protests. She cried and she struggled, but the women surrounded her and held her arms down. Someone pulled her feet out from under her, and she fell flat.

"Our son likes you," someone yelled. "He will make a good husband. You are a foolish girl if you want to shame your parents by leaving. We were all kidnapped. Stop fighting. We won't let you go."

Word quickly spread through the town that Meerim had been kidnapped and was getting married. Rahat had taken a fine, highly educated girl as a wife, and he would not even have to pay the high price such a girl's parents would surely demand. What a triumph for him!

Meerim's sister arrived at the "wedding" to protest that her sister would never agree to marry this way. Meerim had too many wonderful plans. But it was too late for a protest.

Not until after the wedding were Meerim's parents told, "Your daughter has married our son." But what could they do then? The boy had already slept with her. So although they didn't like the way it happened, Meerim's family resigned themselves to the kidnapping. It was their daughter's fate, they said. And secretly Meerim's mother was pleased that her daughter was married. At last some kind of bride price would be forthcoming. "Many marriages begin this way," she said.

Forced labor, kidnapping, rape—in Kyrgyzstan, these are part of everyday life for women and girls trained from birth to be compliant, subservient and passive. Their place is squarely at the bottom of the social hierarchy. And although Meerim had a university degree, though her sense of individualism was far more highly developed than that of the average Kyrgyz woman, she would not defy her mother's wishes that she stay with Rahat. She would not bring shame to her parents. Once she had become Rahat's sexual intimate, she absolutely could not bring herself to leave him.

Meerim and Rahat were permitted to live in a house adjacent to his parents, rather than in the same house, as Kyrgyz tradition requires. And Meerim was allowed to continue to work at her job. While she is glad for her unusual liberties, she describes her life as difficult and unhappy.

Rahat's kindness quickly melted away, especially after Meerim started to grow large with pregnancy. Her new family is Muslim, and they object to her attending church, reading her Bible and contacting her friends. Today Rahat rarely speaks with Meerim except to belittle her. He spends most of his time away from home.

Throughout the first four years, Meerim suspected Rahat of infidelity. When the evidence was undeniable, she asked him to stop seeing the other woman. "Shut up and accept what I do, because I am not going to change," he told her. "If you don't like this arrangement, leave."

But it was too late. Since Meerim gave birth, there have been no more discussions about Rahat's behavior.

Rahat and Meerim's marriage is like the frozen mountains around their home. They look nice from a distance, but up close the realities are harsh. Although Meerim has a good office job, Rahat works only sporadically, and he spends his evenings out. She wishes for a husband's love and tries to talk with him about their daughter's health and education. He is not interested.

We posed this question to local development workers: "How can we bring the practice of bride-stealing to an end?"

Their answer: "It is up to local women. They are the key. Only when the women begin to see girls as individuals who have value through their intelligence and contributions can things begin to change."

Education and opportunities have some power to push back against tradition and unjust practices. Still, consider Meerim. She had both on her side, and in the end, tradition proved to be stronger.

In his documentary film *The Kidnapped Bride,* Peter Lom documents several actual kidnappings. In an interview Lom shares his frustration that there is not enough of an international outcry against this injustice.

"I couldn't marry my true love," one kidnapped bride states. "Only one in one hundred Kyrgyz girls marries her true love. Our life is kidnapping. Accepting and living on."

11

Girls for Sale

Nepal

*O*nce upon a time, Nima was an innocent little girl.

Once upon a time she watched as her mother toiled in the field, the baby tied to her back. And surely Nima thought, *One day, this will be my life.* Not with sadness, mind you, just with resignation. For although the life she saw was a hard one, it was familiar and predictable, the only life rural Nepali girls know.

Once upon a time Nima could walk outside her thatched-hut home and hold her head up high before the neighbors. She could go to the well to fetch water, maybe even walk to the market, and no one called her nasty or spat at her.

Once upon a time—long, long ago.

Now the innocence is gone from her eyes. She is quick to laugh and tease as she knits hats and fashions bead bracelets, and she certainly is more boisterous than the usually reserved Nepali girls we pass in the street. Yet she is wary in her boldness—always watchful. And in the end, it is her eyes that betray her. Twenty years old, just on the threshold of womanhood, yet Nima's eyes are old and weary from having seen far too much.

We were in Nepal, seeking more ways to effectively intervene on behalf of trafficked girls. The person who could provide us with the most help was a take-charge woman named Shanta, the founder and leader of a group consisting of a handful of brave women and men determined to give trafficked girls the chance for a new life. Besides raising awareness with police, border guards, government officials and hospitals (and calling them to accountability), they intervene on behalf of girls crossing the porous border into India. They are always ready to shelter rescued girls.

So passionate is Shanta about her mission and so respected as an expert in her field that she was invited into Nepal's Parliament to speak on trafficking as well as on other issues concerning girls and women. She also puts action behind her words. When a girl is stopped at the border by a suspicious guard, he knows to call Shanta. When a doctor despairs over an HIV-infected prostitute, he calls Shanta. When the police get tired of kicking around a belligerent prostitute but they are not able to simply release her, they call Shanta. And Shanta always comes.

Because of her efforts and those of her organization, many women and girls have been rescued from sex traffickers and whisked away to safe houses where they receive love and acceptance. They also get counseling and the opportunity to learn a skill that will enable them to support themselves. And because of Shanta and her work, many traffickers are locked behind prison bars.

On our first day in Nepal, we sat on the floor of a safe house, in a circle with the resident girls. Shanta introduced us, but only a few said more than a smattering of words. Why should they trust a couple of strangers? On the second day, we met privately with Nima—under Shanta's protective eye. Nima giggled nervously, moved close to

Shanta—whom she calls "Momma"—and looked everywhere but in our eyes.

"Let me tell you a little bit about my own story," Michele began gently. As she told of growing up with alcoholic parents who fought, then of a father who began molesting her when she was a small child, Nima grew still and pensive. Michele shared how she finally told her mother what was happening, but, unable to bear the truth, her mother packed her bags and left. Nima gasped and her eyes filled with tears. Michele told of growing up with her father, of living with fear and helplessness and abuse. By the time she finished her story, Nima was weeping.

Shaken and wiping her eyes, Nima gulped a deep breath. Then she began her story.

Nepal is one of the poorest countries in the world—an estimated 40 percent of its population lives in poverty. Yet even by Nepali standards, Nima's family was poor. "We had no animals, no money, no food," she said. "When I was five years old, my mother left us."

Nima's father beat her mercilessly, and then when he brought a new wife into the house, she joined in the beatings. Little Nima, bruised and bleeding, looked at her three-year-old sister and decided she had only one option. One night she listened until she heard her father's familiar snores, and she listened longer until her stepmother's breathing grew deep and rhythmic. Then she took her sister's hand and together they tiptoed out the door.

"Run!" Nima whispered to her sister. "Run as fast as you can and keep running!"

When they could run no longer, they walked. By the time the sun cast its rays over the mountain peaks, Nima's little sister was crying with exhaustion. It was then that Nima spied a hollow tree. Quickly she dug out the soft dirt around its roots and made a cave below the hollow.

"There," she said to her sister, "a nice room just your size."

With her little sister snuggled down in the tree room, Nima headed back to a herd of goats they had passed on the path. "Please, goat boy, can I have some milk?" she called out. "It's for my little sister." When the boy hesitated, she begged, "Please? So she won't die?" And although he was not at all convinced, the goat herder allowed Nima to take a small amount of milk in an old cup. She sipped a tiny bit, but most of the milk she took back to her sister.

Sheltered in the hole under the tree, Nima and her sister managed to survive on what milk she could beg—or steal. Little sister complained about bug bites on her legs, which she scratched constantly, but what could Nima do? She was only five years old.

Then one morning as the little girls lay sleeping, curled up together, their nest was discovered by a group of men. They were pulled out of the hole, and once the dirt was brushed off them, everyone gasped at the sight of the little one's infected legs.

"I will take her and see that she is made well," one of the rescuers said as he picked up Nima's sister. "My wife and I will adopt her."

"And me too!" Nima cried. "Take me too!"

"No," came the reply. "You will just be a weight around our neck."

And so the would-be rescuers strode away, carrying Nima's weeping sister. Nima ran after them, crying and begging, but their legs were long and hers were very short. Soon they had left her far behind and all alone.

Nima took up a fresh tissue and dabbed at her eyes as she told us of her sad journey back home, of the punishments and beatings she endured for daring to run away, of her endless work cleaning and caring for the animals and caring for the smaller children, of more beatings for any mistake, however small. Her stepmother took every opportunity to make it clear she had no love for little Nima.

Many times Nima thought about running away, but then she remembered her would-be rescuers. Even they didn't want her. If she ran away, where would she go? Who would help her?

When Nima was nine years old, her father informed her that he had arranged a marriage for her. Her new husband was older than her father, and she was so miserable that after six months she left him and went back home to even more beatings than before. So hopeless was her life that she considered killing herself. Instead, she ran away again. She would go far, far away, she determined. She had heard talk of crossing the border into India. No one could find her there.

But a child all alone? She was warned that there would be a guard at the border, and he would never let her cross.

As Nima continued her story, she started to wring her hands, wring her hands, wring her hands.

"Come, child, take my hand," Nima said in another voice. She told us that she looked up to see who was talking to her so kindly and it was a *sadhu*—an Indian holy man dressed in a saffron-colored robe—and he was reaching out to her. "Come, I will help you across the border."

Comfortable that surely a holy man would be safe, Nima took the outstretched hand and walked across the border. Once on the other side, the holy man pointed the way to a bus stop and bid her goodbye.

Nima was all alone in a foreign country where she didn't even know the language.

She didn't have to wait long for a bus, and the bus driver was most kind to her. When he saw she was lost and confused, he said, "Come to my house. My wife will give you a job."

A job! What wonderful good fortune! Nima went home with him, and that very day she started cooking and cleaning for his family and helping in his wife's little shop. "I thought that surely now my life would be better," she told us.

The dream of a better life: that's the very thing that drives most young girls across the border into India. But running girls are not difficult for traffickers to spot. With their networks so well organized and so pervasive, trackers quickly set to work. Who would suspect a kindly holy man? Or a friendly bus driver who offers a job to a helpless child? Or a woman who allows a girl to work in her shop?

Long ago slavery was abolished in Nepal, but it's hard to tell, for still today sex slavery flourishes there. Although many women and girls of all ages are hurt by it, the main victims are girls from poor, rural families who are sold into prostitution. Girls like Nima. It is far too easy to traffic them across the 1,500-mile open border with India. A recent UNICEF study estimates that 300,000 Nepali women and girls have been sold into forced prostitution. And each year another estimated 10,000 girls between the ages of nine and sixteen are trafficked from Nepal into India. In Mumbai alone, more than 20,000 Nepali girls enter prostitution annually.

Of course, Nima knew nothing of this. She stayed with the bus driver and his wife for a year. How could she possibly know she was actually being groomed and trained for what was to come? From the bus driver's house she went to work for an old woman, where she picked tea leaves and learned her ABCs—and where her "training" continued. There were a couple of other places too, but her voice trailed off and it was difficult to follow Shanta's soft translation.

"I thought I was free," Nima said, "and I liked it."

But there was much Nima did not understand. Such as the lovely, flattering words the boys told her before they lay down beside her in her bed. She wasn't even sure how old she was when she became a prostitute. But her training obviously served her well, for the brothel madam set her up in an apartment, and she provided her with servants and gave her new clothes and lavished her with jewelry. She even had her own driver to take her to secret meetings. A rich, influential man sought her out. A government official too. Even a policeman.

"Watch out," an Indian man had warned her as he lay beside her. "This is not a good life for you. You should marry me and leave here. I will marry you anytime you want." Nima shook her head sadly at this recollection. For not too long afterward, when she learned she was pregnant, she sought out that Indian man and insisted he marry her as he had promised. But he laughed and walked away from her. He was already married.

Suddenly Nima went from wealthy, busy and sought-after to poor, jobless, pregnant—and alone. No one wanted her, including the brothel madam.

"I decided to jump into a well and drown myself," Nima said. "But first, I had something to do."

Although her voice was steady and firm, Nima shifted nervously and stared down at the floor. The something she purposed to do was kill the Indian man who had promised to marry her. Nima telephoned him and asked him to meet her at the border station. He agreed and booked a room for her, "since you will be arriving on the train late at night," he said. But once again the man tricked her. He had arranged for two other men to burst into her room and attack her. Though she kicked and screamed, they dragged her off to yet another room. One was just raising a knife to kill her when the police forced their way in and stopped him. The police took the man with the knife away, but they also arrested Nima.

That night Nima slept on the filthy floor of the police station. When she asked the policemen to please let her go, they responded by stealing her only two possessions: a ring and a necklace. She begged them for mercy. They beat her and tossed her into a dark dungeon.

Abuse, abuse and more abuse. According to Shanta, the police are more likely to arrest the girls than to rescue them.

Nima told us that after two weeks in prison, a policeman overheard her speaking in the Nepali language. Since he was also from Nepal, he took pity on her and called Shanta.

At this point in her story, Nima's eyes filled with tears. "Shanta came, and she hugged me and massaged my back," she said in little more than a whisper. "Then she brought me with her to the recovery home in Kathmandu. Shanta loved me, and she tried her best to teach me about love. But it is hard to understand love when no one has ever loved you in your whole life."

At the recovery house, Nima's daughter was born. "And then at last I could understand love."

We like to have our stories end with "and they all lived happily ever after." But that only happens in fairy tales. Trafficking in Nepal is a harsh reality of life. And in a harsh life, girls in Indian brothels are likely to become infected with HIV (as high as 70 percent, according to some estimates). Nima knows many girls who are infected. She worries that she may be too.

"I love my daughter so much," Nima said. "I thank God that she has a good life." Her baby was adopted out of the country by a Christian family.

"No one should suffer the way we have suffered," Nima said. "For the rest of my life, I want to go to the poor and to little girls who are used and abused and help them. I want them to know their lives are too important to mess up."

Nima, like many rescued girls, is already actively at work in a neighboring village, raising awareness about the evils of trafficking and working to help in the rescue effort. It has been a struggle, though, because support for the girls has been meager and sporadic. Even so, this frontline work has rescued about a hundred girls a year.

Her tears dried, Nima stared beyond us and recalled again that long-ago tree of refuge. "God is my big tree," she said to no one in particular. And then she began to recite from her favorite Scripture, Psalm 1:3, 6:

> He is like a tree planted by the streams of water,
>   which yields its fruit in season
> and whose leaf does not wither.
>   Whatever he does prospers. . . .
> For the LORD watches over the way of the righteous,
>   but the way of the wicked will perish.

12

Throwaway Girls

India

She was about seven years old, the little girl we saw when we went to the makeshift school for street kids that the Dalit women had started with profits from their dairy businesses. Or maybe she was eight. Who could tell? All the kids looked pitifully ragged and skinny, but for some reason our guide stopped in front of that little girl, smiled and asked, "What's your name?"

A normal question. But the girl stared blankly, even when he repeated it in the language in which she had been talking just moments before.

"What's your name, little girl?" he repeated, his voice kind and patient.

The girl stared back. As one of the teachers began to explain that a policeman had just brought her to the school because he had nowhere else to take her, the girl whispered, "I have no name. I am nobody."

The girl was found at the train station, the teacher explained. She had been there so long she could barely remember the day her parents left her, promising to come back with warm food. They never returned. That was years ago.

She survived by begging and by sneaking her skinny hands into pockets and purses. Over the years, people had done all sorts of things to her, but when a strange man tried to force her off the train platform, she grabbed hold of a signpost and held on for dear life, all the while screaming at the top of her voice and kicking for all she was worth. She was a pretty scrappy kid for one so scrawny. She made such a racket that someone called the police, and since they had no idea what to do with her (she was, after all, just one of an endless number of abandoned children at the railway platform), they took her to the Dalit women's school for street kids and left her there.

It is difficult indeed to think of that little girl with no name as fortunate. But the fact is, were it not for her fighting spirit, she would almost certainly have been sold into a brothel before we ever walked into the school that day. According to recent data, there are about 2.8 million prostitutes in India. Mumbai alone claims an alarming figure of more than 100,000 in its 12,000 brothels, according to the Human Rights Watch. And the organization reports that 35 percent are under the age of eighteen. Living in filthy conditions, vulnerable to diseases, these girls have no life left to call their own. Should they be fortunate enough to be rescued, they certainly cannot go back home. They have already been abandoned—or sold.

According to an article on child prostitution by Shanker Sen, past director general of National Human Rights Commission, children are kidnapped, taken directly from parents or thrown into prostitution by means of faked marriages. The girls are moved from place to place to place in order to hide their identities. They come from all over the country to supply countless brothels. And, according to a survey conducted by the Ministry of Human Resources and Development, two-thirds of the girls' families live in poverty. Sixty percent of them are Dalits or tribal peoples.

The little girl with no name is unique only in the poignancy of her statement. Children are abandoned every day at India's train stations and bus stops and on city streets. Five-year-old Poonam is another one of them.

Poonam's mother and father took her and her nine-year-old brother on a train trip to Bangalore, but when the family arrived, the mother and father tricked their children into waiting on the platform, then went around behind and got aboard another train that sped away. Perhaps as the parents sat back in their seats, they comforted themselves with the thought that at least their little girl wasn't alone; she had her brother to care for her.

"It was an accident," Poonam's brother insisted to his sobbing sister. "We must have fallen asleep, and we didn't come when they called us. They will be back for us."

Of course, their parents never came back. But Poonam's brother did care for her. He watched out for her, and each day he made certain that she had something to eat. Until he took sick, that is. Then there was no more food for either of them. There was no medical care either. With Poonam beside him, he died on the train platform where his parents had left him.

With growing desperation, Poonam watched the swarms of ragged children begging from people who got on and off the trains. She tried to do the same, but she wasn't very good at it. Again and again, she grabbed hold of some woman's hands and tearfully begged, "Will you take me with you? Please? Please?" But each one pushed her away. No one wanted the filthy little girl.

Because she had no choice, Poonam learned to scavenge through trash cans for bits of chapattis to eat and chicken bones to suck. She became especially skilled at searching under train seats for coins she could use to buy food.

Not yet six, Poonam was an official member of India's burgeoning population of train-platform children—some abandoned, others runaways escaping abusive homes.

Platform children, who range in age from five to fifteen, easily slip on and off trains as the trains constantly move crowds of people between cities in India. Children rarely get checked for a ticket, and if they do, they can easily pass themselves off as beggars. They can get off at any railway station, then get on another train whenever it suits them—or when they get chased off the platform. They are hard to catch because the trains continually move them back and forth throughout the country.

At first, Poonam hung back by herself, too shy and frightened to compete with the aggressive children. But it didn't take her many hungry days to realize that approach wasn't a good one. To survive, she did what most platform children do: she moved in closer to others living on the trains, and soon she joined one of the gangs.

Because the others had survived on the platforms longer than she had, Poonam watched them and learned from them. Soon she, too, was able to get money. No longer did she sleep outside in the rain. She discovered how to approach people in ways that would not irritate them or cause them to shoo her away. When her gang made itself too much at home on the trains and got thrown off, she learned to slip back onto the platform. And when the police came and forced them off the platform, she followed the others as they jumped onto the next train. The kids who had been around knew which trains emptied their cars at what time, and Poonam followed the others as they swarmed onboard to scoop up leftover food from the seats and floor.

During one of the first forays, a boy next to Poonam stuffed his mouth with the remains of a scrambled egg sandwich, but with his other hand he scooped up a torn chapatti doused with lentils and handed it to Poonam. In the gang, the stronger make it their business to look out for the weaker.

With so many platform kids, and more joining them by the day, the number of hungry children far outstrips the amount of food tossed away in trash cans. And with more and more little beggars swarming after them, travelers grow less and less sympathetic toward their plight. Simply to keep from starving, most girls eventually succumb to the advances of sexual predators.

In a pioneering program by Oasis India, rescued platform children now work as counselors to other children on the streets and platforms. This allows the very ones who best know the ins and outs of living on the streets and railway platforms to be on the lookout for children who may be too wary to trust an unknown adult.

Remembering her brother's assurance that they were accidentally forgotten on the train, Poonam once whispered to her gang, "I will find a way to go back home. My mother will be so pleased to see me. She will be sad about my brother, but she will be happy to see me."

The other girls roared with laughter. "You are a fool, Poonam," they said. "Even the police cannot take you home, because your parents probably moved somewhere just so you can't find them. Don't you understand? Your parents left you because they don't want you."

Most likely that was exactly what happened. Families such as Poonam's move all the time.

And what of children rescued from such a life? Most states provide homes for the boys. Several organizations operate homes for them as well. So the boys do have options.

For the girls, it's a different story. When we told the director of a large, secular Indian organization about Poonam, she shook her head and said they are overwhelmed with girls just like her.

"What do you see as her future?" Kay asked.

The woman shook her head sadly. "Girls like her . . . most of them either spend a short, violent life on the platforms, or they end up in the brothels. Some are rescued, but with the exception of a few humanitarian organizations, we have no place for them to go. Most are confined to a room for the rest of their lives."

Institutionalized for life. For the sins of their parents. And of society. And of humanity.

Step Out and Take Action Against Sexual Abuse

*T*his issue makes some of us especially incensed. We simply cannot sit quietly, knowing that someone would exploit a child as a sex slave, or force a girl to marry, or extort sex from a starving girl. If you can't sit still for it, this may be the issue meant for you. To feel empowered rather than immobilized, start by following the steps below.

- Become culture-conscious. Read about the challenges and practices of other peoples so you can understand and explain how our excesses and practices contribute to global evils.

- Join a coalition against abuse in your community. People who care about the issue in the United States will learn from you that there are many countries where victims have little recourse.

- Share <www.usgovinfo.about.com/library/weekly/aa020199.htm>, which tells how to write appropriate letters to legislators, urging sexual abuse interventions.

- Organize a "Resist the Darkness of Abuse Day" at your church or in your community. Choose one Sunday a year to raise awareness about the abuse and exploitation of girls.

- Sponsor a silent auction or golf outing to raise awareness and funds to be used to free and restore victims of trafficking in Nepal.

- Pray for officials in countries such as India to aggressively pursue and prosecute handlers, madams and pimps who prey on impoverished girls.

- Support the young women who have gone from abuse into rescuing young girls in their own country.

- Put a pinned-together, ragged blue dress on display on a bulletin board along with a Resist the Darkness poster, which can be found at <www.resistthedarkness.org/docs/RTDPoster.pdf>.

- Sponsor a movie night to raise awareness of the sexual abuse issue. Charge admission and use the funds to help restore girls.

- Lease a billboard facing a major street and share the message "Abused, abandoned, enslaved . . . just because they are girls" with Sisters In Service's contact information (see pages 176-77).

- Add the Resist the Darkness of Abuse widget to your MySpace page.

- Design a protest T-shirt and e-mail a photo to us.

- Pray for local people such as Shanta who are on the frontlines of the fight against sex trafficking.

- Encourage your church or small group to hold a sale of fair-trade goods and earmark the money for one of the causes in this section. Let people know that fair trade protects people from slave labor.

- Pray for the girls and women entangled in prostitution in your own city. Ask God's leading for those leaders who work with this problem daily, especially those who minister in Christ's name.

PART 4

FREEDOM IN LIFE

*T*en-year-old Lydia hates war. Being a displaced person is miserable. It makes her sad to think of her village so far away from the scorching, sand-blown refugee camp where she has spent the past four years of her life.

"Do trees grow where you live?" she asked us. "My village had green trees. My mother lived there, and she can remember when no one wanted to kill us."

War weighs heavily on everyone, but once again it is the children who pay most dearly. In fact, certain categories of young ones are so vulnerable that they require special advocacy and careful protection if they are to survive and thrive. These include girls, refugees and displaced children. Lydia fits in all three categories.

Thirty-five to forty percent of Iraqi displaced persons are children.

Lydia lives in the war-shredded country of Sudan, where the past two

> "Schools are to be respected as zones of peace."
>
> RADHIKA COOMARASWAMY, UN SPECIAL REPRESENTATIVE FOR CHILDREN AND ARMED CONFLICT

decades have brought most of the population to ruin and destitution. She is by no means alone in her longing for peace.

- By 2002, half a million children had died from sanctions-related causes in Iraq.

- The so-called "Lord's Resistance Army" has abducted about twenty thousand children as child soldiers or sex slaves in Uganda.

- By the turn of the twenty-first century, fifteen thousand Liberian children still carried guns.

- In Uganda and the Republic of Congo, girls are captured and held as forced "bush wives."

- In Iraq, schools are considered "collateral damage" and have been known to be purposely targeted.

- In Rwanda, Uganda, Congo, Sudan and Iraq, there is ample evidence of the sexual violation and torture of girls and women.

Data shows that of all war-affected children, help most frequently bypasses girls, even though victimized girls are the very ones most in need of care. Stigmatized and ostracized by their communities, they are left to struggle alone.

Yet freedom does not simply mean the absence of war. In some places, girls and women are imprisoned even for the "crime" of being victimized.

> "I want to tell the world, 'Please stop fighting. Please, everyone get along.'"
>
> LYDIA

> Remember those who are in prison, as though you were in prison with them; those who are tortured, as though you yourselves were being tortured. (Hebrews 13:3 NRSV)

13

Behind Prison Bars

Pakistan

*W*ere you to meet Kaia, the first thing you would notice is that she could be a serious contender in any beauty contest. The second is the way her eyes flash with anger at injustice. We appreciated her loveliness, but it was her passion for advocacy that drew us to her when we first met at a home meeting. Kaia couldn't wait to address some of the issues we had raised in our first book, *Daughters of Hope*.

"You know, dear sisters," she said, "you were absolutely correct when you wrote that women in Pakistan suffer. But something else is also true. Young girls are languishing in our Pakistani prisons for the crime of being victims and asking for help."

Kaia continued. "It's true, girls and women are caught in a web of helplessness. My father is a lawyer in Pakistan, and he just recently defended a twelve-year-old girl named Majeeda." Then she told us Majeeda's story.

Like many rural girls from impoverished Pakistani families, Majeeda's parents saw no reason to waste their daughter's time in school.

A couple of years of education was plenty. It made much more sense to hire her out to a wealthy family as a day laborer.

Late one day, Majeeda was on her way home after many hours of work in the fields when a man came out of nowhere, forced her behind a tall mound of grain and overpowered her. Majeeda fought and kicked and screamed, but she was no match for the man. Her screams did raise an alarm, however, and other men hurried over to see what was happening. What they saw was their coworker raping Majeeda.

When he finally let her go, Majeeda ran home and sobbed out the whole story to her parents. But, terrified and ashamed, they trembled at the very idea of going to the police to bring a complaint. "What will those witnesses say?" they worried. "Yes, they know what happened. Yes, they saw it all. But would they actually side with a girl? Would they testify against their friend and coworker?"

And yet, when Majeeda's parents considered the terrible thing done to their daughter, they gathered up the courage to go to the police. "Not only did the police refuse to look into the matter," Kaia told us, "but they immediately arrested Majeeda and locked her up in prison. They accused her of making false accusations and of having illegal sexual contact. They said she admitted it."

Kaia continued, "In Pakistan, it is the judge who interprets the level of punishment for sexual crimes. Laws are not applied fairly. Men are presumed innocent, and woman and girls are presumed guilty. And that is not all. A woman's or girl's testimony is not even admissible in Pakistani court."

One judge stated, "Women and girls without counsel will rot in jail."

Imagine being locked up and confused and accused, with no idea of how to go about getting legal representation, and even if you could get help, no money to pay for it. "It is not uncommon for someone to be held for more than a year without even seeing a judge, simply because they don't know how to ask for their day in court," Kaia said.

The vast majority of Pakistan's female prisoners are poor and illiterate. But then, that definition applies to most of Pakistan's female population. According to the government-sponsored Commission on Women, Pakistan has one of the lowest female literacy rates in the world. Only 16 percent are functionally literate, compared to 35 percent of the men.

"What will happen to Majeeda in prison?" Michele asked.

Certainly Pakistan's prisons are of great concern to human rights organizations. In fact, the current Human Rights Report on Pakistan shows that children are detained along with adults and that the guilty awaiting trial are housed together with repeat offenders. Close to three-quarters of the female detainees report sexual abuse at the hands of guards and police.

"She could not fight off that one man," Kaia said sadly. "How can she fight off the other prisoners and the guards as well?"

"If Majeeda is found guilty, what could happen to her?" Michele asked.

Sentences handed down for capital adultery and fornication are severe: up to twenty-five years in prison, one hundred lashes with a whip and a heavy fine. Sometimes, a judge will even order an amputation.

"That is for Majeeda," Kaia said, her eyes flashing with anger. "It is not likely for her attacker though. The sentences usually fall most harshly on females. Muslim men see it as their duty to protect one another, which means the required witnesses won't testify against the man."

The most vulnerable among us . . . Surely no one could be more vulnerable than a poor, illiterate girl in Pakistan.

"A poor, illiterate girl in Pakistan who is a Christian," Kaia said. "Fewer than 2 percent of the people in our country are Christians. For them, life is especially dangerous."

Kaia told of a sinister trend in which a Muslim man will abduct a Christian girl, arrange a "quick marriage," then assign her a Muslim name. From then on, the girl will be his wife, a Muslim and the family's domestic slave.

"She can even be sold," Kaia said. Then she told us the story of another Pakistani girl.

Eleven-year-old Alira's parents already had a young man from a good Christian family in mind for their daughter to marry one day. But all their plans were destroyed when their daughter suddenly disappeared. Right away, they feared she had been abducted. But what could they do? If they went to the police, the child's honor and the family's reputation would be compromised. They could forget about her ever marrying into a good family. So Alira's mother went from neighbor to neighbor asking, "Have you seen my daughter?"

The neighbors matter-of-factly informed her that Alira was now married. And, oh yes, her parents would not be allowed to see her again because they were Christians and she was now a Muslim.

By paying the bribes Alira's husband's family demanded, her parents got one concession: a copy of her marriage certificate. It listed their girl as eighteen years old. And no longer was her name Alira. It had been changed to reflect her forced conversion to Islam.

"Do we have to just forget Majeeda and Alira and all the others like them?" Michele asked Kaia in anguish. "Can't anyone do anything to help them?"

"My father can," Kaia told us. "He works with a group called CLAAS that not only arranges shelter for those who need it but provides them with free legal representation. It also supports them as they continue their education. This group has given many girls a new start in life."

It sounded wonderful, but it also sounded dangerous for the workers—a quick way to make enemies in high places.

"It is very dangerous work," Kaia said. "But it's worth the risk. Our offices in Pakistan were attacked recently. My own father, too, while taking Samira to a safe house—"

"Samira? Who is Samira?"

"I didn't tell you about Samira?" Kaia said. "She's a girl from a Christian family who was abducted by a Muslim man and held for sixteen days. She was forced to convert to Islam and to go through a marriage ceremony, and then she was raped. After weeks of mistreatment, she managed to escape back to her parents' house. But when her neighbors found out what had happened, they attacked the house and demanded that she go back to her husband. Samira's parents didn't know what to do. Fortunately they called my father and he hurried over. With the help of coworkers, he managed to get Samira into the car, but as they drove away, the mob of neighbors attacked them. They smashed in the front windshield, and the car swerved off the road and crashed. But before the mob could attack again, a police car drove up."

Samira's "husband" demanded that she be returned to him—in accordance with the law. And Pakistani law was indeed behind his claim. Even so, in the end Samira's CLAAS lawyers defeated his legal demand.

Some of Pakistan's youngest captives are finally being set free.

14

Surviving War

Sudan

*I*n the best of times, Sudan is a harsh, inhospitable land. These are far from the best of times. Yet the searing heat and blowing sand are not the reasons we count it among the hardest places we visit. Nor is it because of the suspicious eyes of heavily armed guards who constantly follow us as we make our way to interview displaced women and girls. No, Sudan is hardest because of the difficult questions we encounter there.

"Do our brothers and sisters in the West know what's happening to us? Do they know we are being forced from our villages? That we are being raped and killed?"

Yes, we say, they know. The plight of the Sudanese is reported in newspapers and shown on television, and it saddens and horrifies us.

"If everyone knows," they say, "where are God's people who have freedom? Why don't they help us?"

That's why Sudan is the hardest place. Yet we go anyway, because the more God's people know, the more they care.

We tried to get the necessary documents to go into Darfur, but once again we were denied access to that distressed area. So we decided to do the next best thing: we interviewed Dorcas, a Sudanese coworker who ministers to the women in the camps, and with their permission, she shared the stories of Amina and Khadijah.

"My name is Amina, and I am Furian, from Darfur. When I was a small child of six or seven, I lost my parents because they were dragged away by the armed men who attacked our village. They were taken to a place I did not know. I hid that night so I would not be captured too. It looked to me that all my family was killed. I have no idea, even until now, where they are, but I heard that everyone captured that night was thrown into a dry well."

Numb with horror, little Amina moved along with a group of other survivors desperate to escape that nighttime attack. They helped each other to keep moving.

"We struggled together to reach a path that could take us to a safer area. We were lucky to reach a petrol station with trade vehicles that would transport us. The drivers were ready to leave immediately for the city of Nyala.

"We traveled four nights before we finally arrived at a town outside of Nyala. I stayed there almost two years, but then we were attacked again. This time I had to run away alone. I got lost and could not find my way back. As I wandered around, armed men abducted me. For three months they held me captive, forcing me to cook for them and wash their clothes. They tortured me and raped me. All nine men, again and again.

"Other girls and women moved with the group too. They treated all of us like donkeys. Every day they raped some of us. One time I could not endure it, and I fainted as they raped me. One of them hit me, and when I couldn't respond normally, they all beat me and beat me.

"One day the men all left the camp, and the girls were left alone with one of the gunmen. He was exhausted, so after a while he fell into a sound sleep. Three of us looked at each other, and without saying any words, we made a decision: it would be better to die than to stay with those men."

For a day and a half the girls ran, with no water and no food. Just as they were ready to drop, they met a group of nomadic herders who were moving their animals to the market. The herders listened sympathetically as the bedraggled girls poured out their story, then they gave them water and food.

"We went with the herders to Nyala, where we reported to a displaced persons camp," Amina said. "We thank God we are girls. If we had been men, the soldiers would have killed us."

Even though Sudan is the hardest place for us, we keep going back. And right here you can see why. In the midst of overwhelming suffering and despair, Sudanese Christians point us to the hand of God. They look through the blowing sand and beyond the unbearable horror, and they offer seeds of blessing and hope.

"I am Khadijah. At sixteen, I married a soldier. When he was away for duty, I stayed with his family. I had two children and was newly pregnant. One night the village where we stayed was suddenly attacked. We were forced to move, not to another town, but toward a remote village. But just as we were awakening the next morning, gunmen arrived and burned the village where we rested. Almost all the men were killed. Women who refused to obey the armed men were also killed, and so were the children who clung to them.

"We were captured. For fear of death, we went along and most of our children were spared. But not mine. They got left behind as I was dragged away by a brutal man who would not listen to their cries.

"The men bit us, and we have scars on our bodies to show it. They dragged us into the wilderness where we were to sleep, then the chief gunman ordered his soldiers to divide us among themselves. We did not fight because our sisters who resisted were chopped by machetes or shot dead. To my shock, those of us who looked youngest or pregnant were raped by several men even before we spent the first night. I was so tired I wished they would just kill me.

"Days and days passed. I grew sick and could only live with sadness of rape day and night. I begged the chief to have me killed. I told him I could no longer bear it even one more time. Only then was I kept under his care for five months, living among his six wives and young children.

"Finally someone took pity on me, and I was escorted out from that place. I found my way to a camp where I received treatments, and now I am better. But I have no husband. I struggle to survive. Maybe my real husband will appear one day and take me back home.

"I found my cousin Asha at the camp. Her husband was killed in the attacks. She had two children with her, and she was pregnant and had no place to go, so they all stayed with me, even though it was so hard to get enough food for so many mouths.

"One time we were busy collecting firewood when a man carrying a load of sticks came up to Asha. We were frightened of him, and we started to run. But my cousin fell down and before she could get up again, he reached her. I heard Asha screaming, pleading with the man not to rape her because she was already close to delivering her baby. But he did what he wanted to do.

"I was so frightened I could not run from my hiding place. The man and Asha were so close I could hear the screaming and all the other sounds. If he had come forward only a little bit, he would have found me and killed me. I was so horrified and scared that even when I could no longer hear a sound, I stayed for a long time.

"Finally I forced myself to get up and walk back to camp. When I told my neighbors what had happened, many took courage and went back to look for Asha. They found her killed with her stomach cut open. We mourned and mourned for Asha and her baby. When we could mourn no more, we buried them in that awful place.

"Asha's children are with me now, and so is my newborn baby. We still mourn for my cousin. When will our suffering end? Will these children ever find favor with people of goodwill who will help them go to school? We don't know.

"We continue to struggle. And we hope for peace to prevail.

"Will you help us? Please! Will you help us?"

Dorcas and her team of strong Sudanese women do what we long to do but cannot. They ride donkeys directly into those areas of horror. They listen as the girls pour out their stories. They bring needed food and blankets. They come with tender, accepting embraces and the restoring love of God.

"We invite them to come to our center for women," Dorcas told us. "We can still take a few more who want to learn a skill and build a new life. We also provide free school for some of the children, but there is no money to pay the teachers. We don't know how long they can continue to go home to their own children with no money for food. But news is spreading that God loves the Fur people. And that news brings great hope. Darfur is responding to Christ!"

But then the questions come from Dorcas too: "Do our brothers and sisters know what is happening to us? Can they hear our cries? If they care, why do they not help us?"

15

Sisters of War

Iraq

*A*lina waited on the edge of the ophthalmologist's examination table, just as she had many times before. She knew he would try to sound positive, but she mustered her faith for any outcome. *I have seen so many things in my nineteen years,* she thought. *If I must go through life seeing nothing more, by God's grace I can still be used by him.*

Instead of focusing on the upcoming examination, Alina concentrated on remembering all the things she had already been privileged to see. Despite the constant conflict—war with Iran, Desert Storm and now another war—she had seen the beautiful blue sky, snow, fields of poppies, the faces of her family and friends. *I have so many memories to treasure,* she thought.

As a preschooler, Alina had seen her father off to war. Every few months he would come home for a weekend. And such a father— kind, and so passionate about his faith. One time he said, laughing, "Just imagine, I was praying to God to save me while enemy pilots were praying to hit their target—me!" Sure, she had seen the various struggles her parents had endured, yet they never succumbed to bitterness or hatred. It was their courage that always brought her home for strength whenever she needed peace.

Alina had watched her mother carry on family life with dignity, courage and hard work. Tanks, shells and ruined buildings were as common to Alina as a playground might be to girls in the United States.

So, what do you do when surrounded by continual war and violence? You decide what kind of person you will be in the midst of it. This was the attitude Alina saw displayed by her family. And what they decided to do was make a difference by serving and helping others.

When Alina's father finished his mandatory military service, the family tried to resume normal life. Her parents are intelligent and educated, so they had great opportunities to build a good life for their family. They had a nice home, plenty of food, good schools and friends.

However, it hurt them terribly to see the hatred poured out on the Kurdish people who lived near their neighborhood. The Kurds had never been treated well and were always denied jobs, but as Saddam's government began targeting them, things grew much worse.

"I saw my parents begin to reach out with the love of God to the poor people living in shantytowns," Alina said. "My father would take food and blankets to their communities and try to share God's love with them."

Alina was not the only one who saw it. A friend of the family came to their home and warned, "Do not get too involved with Kurds. It is dangerous for your family."

Things grew worse quickly. Neighbors were not happy about this friendliness with Kurds. Alina remembered one terrible night in particular: "We heard loud thumping on the side of our house. My little brother and I looked out the window and saw our neighbors yelling and throwing rocks. Even our playmates were caught up in the anger against us. We could see it in their faces. I will never forget how my brother looked at me with terror and disbelief. He began to shake, and for many months he didn't speak. We had to leave that house.

Friends in another town allowed us to hide in their home while my parents decided what to do."

They found another place to live, but their trouble didn't end. When the Kurdish area was attacked with poison gas, Alina's father dared to help shelter them. Once again he drew hatred down on his family. Even as many Kurds streamed north in search of safety, an urgent warning came to Alina's father: "You are being watched. You must never again have contact with Kurds. If you do, no one can protect you."

So, what do you do when you are surrounded by continual war and violence? You decide what kind of person you will be in the midst of it. Alina saw her parents respond by praying for guidance. They were certain they were to continue showing God's love to the Kurds. If the Kurds were leaving for the north, then Alina's family would go as well.

"Each of us can take one small suitcase," her mother instructed.

Their friends thought they had lost their minds. Risk their lives to go to an undeveloped area of Iraq? Where electricity and water systems didn't function? And no decent schools existed for their children? How could they be so foolish!

Alina watched as her parents gladly went. "We felt that our whole family had an assignment and a purpose," she said.

How vividly she could remember that day her family first arrived in northern Iraq. It was cold and the mountains were white. Seven-year-old Alina had never before seen mountains or snow. She and her brother climbed to the top of their roof and gazed out over the entire town.

Alina started first grade in a Kurdish school. Not knowing the language, she spent her first week making hand signs and scribbles on paper in an effort to communicate. But soon she started to pick up words. "I spoke Arabic, which no one seemed to know," she said. "Even the kids who did understand me acted as if they didn't know what I was saying. They had racist sort of feelings against me. I simply had to learn to speak in Kurdish. It took a while, but I had an advantage because I was constantly hearing Kurdish spoken by my classmates around me."

Alina's father started a church and a radio program, and her mother worked with widows and people with disabilities. Alina wanted to be useful too, so she pitched in doing whatever she could to help: sorting books, coordinating a newsletter or helping with the children.

From the time she was a small child, Alina had been full of ideas. That's what her mother said. One year, Alina decided they should teach the Kurdish children about Easter. So she told her mother, "We could boil eggs, color them and give them to the neighbors. When they ask for an explanation, we will have a perfect opportunity to talk about the hope of new life." It worked so well that, long after Easter had passed, neighbor children continued to show up and ask for eggs, which Alina happily continued to distribute.

Like both her parents, Alina was naturally bold. Also, she excelled at science and math. When she and her father decided to have a radio program about math and science just for children, it was Alina's responsibility to create the program and be the on-air instructor every day. For three years, she taught in a way that made learning fun. Kids loved having a program just for them, and many wrote letters telling how much they enjoyed learning. It greatly encouraged Alina's passion to reach out to others.

Alina saw her family's outreach expand to several major cities in the north. And she often joined groups of Christian women who went from town to town, training other women and encouraging them. Anywhere churches and women's opportunities were growing, that's where they went.

They even went into prisons, if that's where hurting women needed them. Alina's mother led the women to speak up for an imprisoned girl named Nisa. Nisa's father was a friendly man, always ready to talk to anyone—even strangers. When Alina's dad stopped by his housewares shop, the two men talked about their families, then about faith. Over time Nisa's entire family started going to the church. They were filled with joy for life and excitement about the good things ahead in their country. Nisa's extended family, however, grew increasingly angry with them.

One afternoon Nisa's uncle stopped by the shop, angry and ready to confront her father. But Nisa's dad was away, so the uncle started yelling at Nisa and her brother about their decision to go to church. He grabbed Nisa and shook her. When she tried to pull free, he slapped her and pushed her backward. When he lunged at her again, Nisa panicked. She covered her face and grabbed for something to defend herself. The next thing she knew, her uncle was on the floor, and she was in the hands of a mob who turned her over to the police. Her uncle died of a head wound. At the age of fourteen, Nisa was tried for murder—as an adult.

Oh, yes, Alina could still see it all: her mother and the women of the church advocating for Nisa to be tried as a minor for the accidental death of her uncle. Securing an attorney to plead her case—for free. Visiting Nisa every day with the women of the church, bringing her food and doing all they could to encourage her.

In three years, Nisa will be released from prison. But when that happens, her vengeful relatives will pose the greatest danger—to her life. So the same women who watch over her in prison will guide her safely to a new life in another town.

Because of Nisa's imprisonment, the awful conditions of women and girls in the prison are no longer a secret. Now a small prison ministry has sprung up where women can minister to women.

It was working in the women's ministry that left Alina wounded.

Travel in Iraq is always precarious. At each of the multiple checkpoints, cars are searched and passengers questioned about the purpose of their travel. Every time Alina saw a charred automobile beside the road, she knew it was the result of yet another blast by yet another hidden explosive. Her father's words were never far from her mind: "This is what it costs to minister in Iraq today."

That was what he had said as he placed a bullet in a small jar on the family coffee table. His best friend, Rahim, had been working in a bookstore and lending library when a man came in and asked for a book. Rahim turned to reach for the book, and the man shot him in the back of the head. Now Rahim's wife is a widow and their children are without a father. Alina's father kept the bullet.

Alina leaned her head back against the smooth wall of the ophthalmologist's office. Once again she could see the old car filled with excited women all talking at once. They were on their way to the Women's Training Center, where each woman had a special contribution to make. But while they were still a few miles away, the rapid staccato of machine-gun fire tore through their chatter, and bullets peppered the car. Each woman screamed for the others to get down as bullets shattered window after window.

Alina was sitting in the middle of the back seat. "I turned around to see why people were lying down," she said. "The mother of two children grabbed her little ones and pushed them to the floor by her feet. Then, in the flash of a second, the back window came flying in toward my head. A painful noise roared in my right ear, and my head ached terribly. Everyone in the car screamed while bullets continued to fly by. We all started praying. Our car swerved in the street, but somehow we got away. I remember yelling, 'I can't hear!'

"When I lifted my head, it was like two black holes were in front of me. The deafening noise was the sound of death rushing by us. But by God's grace, we were spared. Through a blur I could see that my hands were bloody. My right eye felt strange. Glass was all over me, all in my skin. In the hospital they tried to take out all those embedded shards; I definitely remember that."

Even before the day was over, e-mails flew around the world asking for prayer for Alina's eyes. No one knew the extent of the damage, but from the sound of the e-mail, she was blind.

"It was so painful," she said. "Later they discovered a shard of glass, and they were able to safely remove it. Many months later a large piece of glass came through my skin and out my scalp, and I could see again."

The emotional wounds were more difficult to heal than the physical. Ever since that day, Alina has been terrified of helicopter and bullet noises.

But as she waited for the doctor's words, she was calm. "What I can see is that God is in control," she told us. "Even in a situation like ours. Even here, he was watching over us. Thank you for your prayers."

We in the United States feel so far away from our sisters in Iraq—far removed from the bullets, explosions and helicopters. Yet through prayer we can stand beside them and give the most powerful gift of all.

Step Out and Take Action
for Freedom in Life

*E*very person created by God has the right to be free. This includes little girls. None should be imprisoned or captive as a domestic slave or fear reprisals for speaking against an abuser. When we first learned of girls imprisoned in Pakistan for false accusation, we could hardly believe it. But hundreds of pages of documentation and government research confirmed every word. And to think that girls are forced to be slaves to soldiers wherever there is conflict! As much as we love our freedoms, we hope it moves us to demand and work for freedom for girls in developing nations too.

- Write your legislators and encourage them to fight for more money to go toward combating the slavery of girls.

- Book a time slot on your local access TV station to raise awareness about enslaved girls.

- Start a college or community chapter that raises awareness and helps to address all kinds of slavery.

- Help start a walk-a-thon in your city to raise money to restore the lives of enslaved girls.

- Put your freedom to good use by signing up to become a Sisters In

Service spokesperson for girls. E-mail your letter of interest to <info@sistersinservice.org>.

- Talk to businesses in your area about donating a percentage of their sales for a day, a month or a year to intervene for enslaved girls.

- Place an official Resist the Darkness of Exploitation advertisement in a local magazine or newspaper. Download a widget or advertisement at <www.resistthedarkness.org/docs/RTD_Advertisement.pdf>.

- Organize and attend a child-trafficking awareness rally.

- Help organize a competitive event to raise awareness and funds to help girls learn a vocation.

- Discuss the Frontline video *The Kidnapped Bride* with a small group or class. Go to <www.pbs.org/frontlineworld/stories/kyrgyzstan/thestory.html> and click "watch video."

- Carry a photo of a girl from one of these countries in your wallet— along with photos of your loved ones. (Let us know if you need one by e-mailing us at <info@sistersinservice.org>.)

- Organize a musical concert to help Sudan.

- Help fund a prison outreach program in Iraq or Pakistan. If you are interested, contact us at <info@sistersinservice.org>.

PART 5

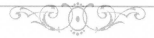

Spiritual Life

From the largest unreached nation (Turkey, according to Operation World; few of its 66 million Muslims have ever heard the gospel) to one of the twentieth century's greatest evangelical success stories (the phenomenal growth of the church in China has no parallel in history), we both rejoice and feel frustrated. In China, the past fifty years have seen a growth in the Protestant church from about 3 million (total of official churches and unofficial house churches) to about 43 million. In the same period, the Catholic Church grew from 3 million to 12 million.

Yet almost 12,000 people groups throughout the world remain unreached with the gospel of Jesus Christ. Of these, more than 4,500—39 percent— live in India. Over the past decade, the persecution of Indian Christians by extremist Hindu groups has steadily increased. Many churches have been burned, and pastors and other Christian

Eighty percent of unreached people are women and children.

> The harvest is plentiful but the workers are few.
>
> (MATTHEW 9:37)

leaders attacked, even killed. Terrified believers hide in the forests until hunger and thirst overcome their terror. Even so, the Indian church continues to increase.

Not so in other countries. Many will be surprised to learn that less than 1 percent of Japan's population is Christian.

In Somalia, East Africa—the world's most lawless country—Christians have been killed, driven out or pushed far underground. In the entire world, the number of Somali Christians is believed to be no more than two thousand.

Yet there are definitely reasons to rejoice, for example:

- Before 1960, no Christian was officially allowed to live in Nepal. Today that country is home to half a million believers.

- Despite its extreme repression and persecution, North Korea's underground church is still alive.

- For a quarter of a century, Sudanese Christians, driven from their homes in the south by an endless war with Sudanese Arabs, have struggled desperately to survive a brutal life as displaced people. Yet they choose to see themselves as missionaries rather than refugees, and because of their witness, thousands of Muslims have come to Christ and churches have been started.

- Ninety-nine percent of the world's people are potentially able to hear the gospel via Christian radio in a language they can understand.

In the previous chapters, we have seen God's hand at work and his love demonstrated by those who minister caringly to the immediate holistic needs of the people. You may have noticed that even in the hardest of places, local Christians are already at work. Because they know the language, are part of the culture and live with the same circumstances, local Christians have access and insights to effectively reach their neighbors. And Western Christians have resources and experiences to bring to our shared task of extending the gospel.

We work best when we all work together, for we are the body of Christ.

"Show me your faith without

deeds, and I will show you

my faith by what I do."

JAMES 2:18

16

An Awakening

Iran

When Michele heard Naseem speak at a luncheon about her work in Iran, she knew immediately that this was a woman with whom we needed to meet. Naseem had the stories we longed to hear.

Naseem was gracious to us, but from the beginning she had a difficult time with our interview. She confessed as much: "You must not speak against anyone's religion. It is not that I don't want to tell you the stories. But how can I be certain you will not put anyone at risk? Can you absolutely assure me?"

Naseem has good reason to fear. A quick Internet survey on Iran finds extremism and conditions that raise concerns for women and girls—actually, for everyone who lives there. Police sweep through Tehran, looking for anyone who appears "too Western." Women must wear dark layers of loose-fitting clothes, and their hair must be entirely covered. Those who question or resist are arrested on the spot.

A peaceful gathering of women on International Women's Day was met with the brutal arrests of thirty women in a park. After seventeen years in operation, *Zanan,* a popular women's magazine, was closed down because it was "corrupting the culture." And just a month before this writing, a twenty-two-year-old woman was sentenced to five years in prison for participating in an event called "One Million Signatures," which supports greater rights for women. A female student who complained of sexual harassment by a senior male lecturer was also charged, despite the fact that YouTube postings show the woman's fellow students with an audio recording of the lecturer sexually propositioning her. "Publicizing certain crimes is worse than the crimes themselves," the local prosecutor claimed.

The suppression of women and girls creates deadly vulnerabilities, warns Dr. Donna Hughes, professor of Women's Studies at Rhode Island University. "There has been a 635-percent increase in the number of teenage girls in prostitution," she said.

The Social Department of the Interior Ministry of Iran actually proposes "morality houses" and the use of temporary marriage customs in which a couple can marry for a short time, even an hour, to make prostitution easier. This is hard to understand from our Western viewpoint. But Iran is a theocratic republic, 98 percent Muslim, with a strict legal system based on sharia law.

Fixed in the tenth century, sharia law brings together elements from the Qur'an and the Hadith, a collection of the deeds and words of Muhammad, plus judges' rulings from Islam's first centuries. It also establishes such things as the inferior status of women. But what we in the West are most familiar with is its penal code: the prescribed punishments for sexual offenses that include stoning; for theft that include amputation; for apostasy against Islam, for which the punishment is death.

It would seem that the sexual abuse and exploitation of girls is a huge contradiction in a culture that publicly stones and hangs people for any hint of sexual impurity. "Not really," Naseem said. "Girls are considered second-class citizens. Exploitation and repression actually fit right together."

But things are changing in Iran, Naseem told us. Many educated women are pushing for change—carefully, but pushing nevertheless. Then she told us of a far more amazing change: "Many are also turning to Christ."

One of the greatest things about traveling to different places to talk with our sisters in diverse areas of the world is hearing the unexpected and miraculous ways God shows himself. Many times we have sat speechless and amazed as we listened to a girl's or woman's story. We asked Naseen if she could tell us about someone in Iran to whom God had shown himself.

For a long time Naseem was silent. Then she murmured, "There are so many stories like that. Thousands from which I could choose." She sat for several more moments, then said, "I will tell you about Dorri."

Dorri's mother died when Dorri was quite young, and after that the girl was treated poorly. Her father remarried, and her new stepmother seemed to have a particular hatred for the child. She constantly hurled insults at her, beat her and generally made her life miserable.

"At one point, her stepmother started a fire in the house intending to burn Dorri alive," Naseem said. "Dorri barely escaped."

As she grew, Dorri knew for certain she could never be loved. Everything in her life was evidence of that. Rejection cast a shadow over her, and it never lifted. She lived with the echo of her stepmother's words "You are good for nothing!" As soon as Dorri reached adolescence, her family arranged a marriage for her, but that drove her only into deeper despair.

There was a nice park not far from her house, and for long hours Dorri sat there alone, watching the people. How she envied every one of them! One older woman who came often was Nahid, a widow who lived with her son. He greatly admired his mother for her kind ways. "Most women go out of the house with an empty basket, hoping to fill it with fruits and vegetables," Naseem said, mimicking the son's voice. "They shop and then they come home. But you, my mother, go out with a basket full of good things and are only happy when you share everything and the basket is empty."

Nahid's desire was to somehow share God's love with one person each day. She often fasted and prayed, asking God to show her creative ways to accomplish this. Some days she would ride several buses and leave literature in seat compartments. Other days she would walk through the park, praying that God would allow someone to cross her path who was willing to receive what she had to share.

One day Nahid had a great abundance of Christian literature in her basket, all carefully hidden under a layer of apples. How could she find a way to get these "messages of hope" to the most receptive people? God would guide her, of that she was certain. When she arrived at the park, Nahid was amazed to see an extremely large gathering of women. Could it be that God had sent them all in answer to her prayer?

After an entire day of visiting with the women and handing out literature, Nahid was tired, so she sat down with her basket of apples. It felt good to take a break. Suddenly the police started to arrest the women, who had actually gathered in the park to demonstrate for women's rights. When the police got to Nahid, they were especially aggressive.

"I am only sitting here eating apples," Nahid said calmly, despite her growing fear. They grabbed her basket and roughly dug down to the bottom. Panic rose in Nahid. Had she given away all the literature, or was there some still buried under the apples? She couldn't be certain. The police grabbed her basket and turned it upside down, then they grabbed her and shook out the flowing clothing that covered her from head to foot.

Only when the police turned to walk away did Nahid dare to breathe. Imagine if she had not just finished giving away all her literature. God had miraculously protected her.

Another woman was alone in the park that day too. It was Dorri. She wasn't protesting anything, nor was she giving anything away. She was simply watching. In her safe place on the outskirts of the park, she picked up a wrinkled piece of literature and tucked it into the fold of her *chador*, then she went home.

In the safety of her house, Dorri took out the paper, smoothed it and read the words "God is love."

What a strange concept, Dorri thought. *God is creator. God is judge. But God is love? Could that be true?*

Dorri's heart beat faster. Could God love her? She had to find out.

Not too long after, Dorri went with her husband on a business trip outside the country. They were invited to a gathering of Iranians who turned out to be Christians, and there she heard the amazing message again: "God is love. He loves every person he created. He sent his son to die for your sins." The pastor who spoke invited people to talk to him after his message.

Reluctantly Dorri and her husband made their way up to him. "We don't want to receive this message," Dorri's husband insisted. "But would you pray with us anyway?"

In that moment, Dorri's life changed forever. As the couple prayed, she gladly received God's love in Christ. In time, her husband did the same.

"You would not believe the change in Dorri," Naseem told us. "Only God could change someone the way she was changed. She is confident and joyful, truly a bold minister of God's love in one of the largest churches, though I dare not tell you where."

They need to stay hidden. We had heard about secret believers in Iran, but had no idea how many.

"Thousands," Naseem said. "The church in Iran is experiencing tremendous growth. But great growth increases the chance of persecution. If a Christian's faith is found out, that person can lose their job—or worse. One woman very close to me was head nurse at a hospital until someone discovered she was a Christian. After that she was systematically demoted. Finally a friend urged her to resign before she lost her pension. She did, but it made her so sad to no longer do the work she loved."

It is no surprise to hear that the underground church in Iran endures many pressures. But we rejoice to hear about the many miracles it is experiencing too.

"Jesus is so attractive, especially to women," Naseem told us. "The way he received women, showing them respect and kindness, is something women here deeply desire. His treatment of the woman caught in adultery touches them. This is like no other religious teacher they've heard."

"What about the girls?" Michele asked.

"Pray that they will find suitable Christian husbands," Naseem said. "Many more women and girls are in underground churches than men. Pray, too, that they will be able to start small businesses to support themselves. Pray that they will learn that they are human beings who should be treated with respect. Most Iranian girls have never been taught about their value, and they bring their inferior feelings about being females into their new faith. Even after they come to Christ, many bury their talents instead of using them."

Not all, though. A growing number of Iranian Christian women are amazingly active and bold despite the repression. One very talkative Christian woman, Sima, placed a telephone call to her friend Maria. Hardly taking a breath, she said, "I just wanted to tell you I was praying for your daughter who is so ill. God encouraged my heart, and I am certain she will be well! . . . Please don't cry. . . . Maria, why are you sobbing?"

And that's when a man's voice broke into the conversation on the other end of the telephone line. "My wife cannot talk anymore. You have reached the wrong number. Goodbye."

Did I dial the wrong number? Sima thought in confusion. *The person answered to Maria, and that certainly is not a common name in Iran.*

The next day Sima received a call from the same man. *Oh, no!* Sima thought. *I got the wrong "Maria" into terrible trouble!*

"I had to call you back today," the man said. "We have never heard of anyone in our country with the same name as my wife. But your words gave her great comfort. Our teenage daughter is a drug addict. My wife had the best night of sleep she's had in years. We want to talk to you about some of the things you said. Could you and your husband meet us for tea?"

17

From Daughter of a Geisha
to Daughter of the King

Japan

*G*od knows everything about us from the time we are born," says Yoshi. "From the beginning, he has a plan to accomplish through us." This is an interesting statement from a girl who grew up knowing all about women being used, a girl raised with abuse who never knew love from her mother.

To understand Yoshi's story, we need to back up two generations, to the time her grandmother—whom we will call Haru—was a child. Haru's father had six daughters, a strong taste for alcohol and with little money. He lessened the pressures in his life by selling young Haru to a geisha house. She would become a classy prostitute.

At the age of sixteen, Haru gave birth to a baby we will call Keiko, then she traded that baby to Ai, the geisha house owner, in exchange for forgiveness of her debts. This was a good deal for Haru; she was now debt free. And a good deal for Ai; she had a baby girl she could raise to be a geisha. A terrible deal for little Keiko; she was a business transaction from birth.

Keiko, who grew to be Yoshi's mother, was loved by no one. Scrubbing floors in the geisha house kept Keiko busy during the day, but at night she watched the beautiful geishas go out dressed in gorgeous kimonos. They came back late, laughing and reeking of alcohol and eager to count their money.

"Money," Keiko whispered to herself, "that's what brings happiness."

The geisha house owner knew geisha life would not last forever in Japan, so she told Keiko she must get an education. But where is the money in learning? Keiko thought. So at the age of nine, already determined to become a top geisha and earn more money than any of the others, Keiko ran away and joined another geisha house.

Keiko did become a geisha—beautiful, but not topnotch. She did go out at night dressed in a gorgeous kimono, and she did come back laughing and filled with drink, eager to count her money. But it didn't bring her the happiness she expected.

When Keiko was twenty years old, an extremely wealthy businessman chose her to be his personal mistress. It was the answer to every geisha's dream. "I think he really did love my mother," Yoshi said of the businessman who was her father. "She was very beautiful."

Keiko loved the businessman for what he could give her: security, money and, most of all, power. To her, he was simply a smart business deal.

"When I was born, my father made my mother quit the geisha house," Yoshi said. "He told her, 'You are a mother now, and you need to be with your daughter. I will give you the money you want.'" Keiko happily took the businessman's money, but she had no intention of staying home.

At that time, everything was changing in Japan. A population raised to obey, to do as they were told without question, had just lost the war. Devastated and humiliated, they watched as General Douglas MacArthur marched in, bringing new ways of doing things. This included ending legalized prostitution, which meant much less business in geisha houses. Because she saw her profits plummeting, Ai accepted Yoshi's father's invitation to come to live with Keiko and care for her baby while Keiko spent her days shopping.

Keiko had no love for Ai, who her child would grow to call Granny. And Ai had no love for Keiko. But Granny did love baby Yoshi, and Yoshi loved Granny. "We were best friends," Yoshi said. "Each morning I sat next to her, and we prayed to the Buddhist god. It was my job to bring the offering of a bowl of rice and water. Granny would ring the bell, and we would hold hands and bow. Then she would start chanting, the same words over and over. She had no idea what she was saying. Just the same chant, twice every day, 365 days a year."

Because little Yoshi wanted to please her Granny, she mumbled the lines along with her. And when the two of them went on walks together and paused at the shrines on every corner, she helped to ring the bells. "We did that to wake the gods," Yoshi said.

Yet even though she was raised by Ai, who greatly believed in Buddhist prayers and ancestors who were strong protectors, Yoshi never did believe. "So many times I went to the shrine to pray for good grades," she said, "but I still wasn't a good student. There was too much chaos in my house for me to study, so my prayers weren't answered. I prayed for peace in my house too, but that wasn't answered either. Mostly I prayed because I feared the ancestors would come after me if I didn't. And since I was taught to believe in reincarnation, I was afraid I might come back as an animal or a bug if I didn't pray."

Day after day, Granny Ai yelled at Keiko, saying she had always hated taking care of her when she was little and that she had only given Keiko food because she'd had to. And Keiko despised Granny Ai because the woman who never loved her did love Yoshi. It sparked such jealousy that the girl didn't dare hold Granny's hand in front of her mother.

When Yoshi was ten, Keiko decided the businessman was too old for her, so she left him. He died soon after. "My father was the most generous, gracious and compassionate person I ever met," Yoshi said. "I didn't see him often, but he really cared about my mother and me."

Throughout her growing-up years, Yoshi bore the brunt of her mother's cruelty, both emotional and physical. "I never had a good conversation with her," Yoshi said. "She was mean and sarcastic, always accusing me of tattling on her, always telling me I was no good and never did anything right." Then Yoshi added pensively, "That's what happens when a person is raised without love."

During Yoshi's teen years, Keiko opened a coffee shop. Successful at that, she opened a mahjong parlor—a Chinese gambling place. Every morning Keiko was up long before dawn, and she worked in the coffee shop until after dinner, then she donned her kimono and went to work at the mahjong parlor and was there until midnight. She never slept more than three hours, and she never took a day off, because every hour meant more money. When Keiko was at home, she drank liquor and brooded about how terribly people had treated her.

"I lay awake at night and heard plates smashing against the wall and my mother screaming," Yoshi said.

Keiko's unspoken lesson to her daughter was, "Love is nothing, money is everything. Only in money will you find security."

By the age of eighteen, Yoshi gave up hope of finding happiness in Japan. Her mother had always enrolled her in every extra class the neighbor children took (they must never be allowed to get ahead of her!) and her favorite by far was English.

Since junior high school, Yoshi had begged to go abroad to study English for a few months. Finally her mother agreed, though reluctantly. But Yoshi put so much time and effort into English that she neglected her other subjects. To her dismay, she failed the entrance exam. "My dream was shattered," she said. "I just had to get out of that house!"

It was right at the time when Keiko's own fortunes began to plummet. People took notice of her rudeness and mean behavior. One person whispered to another, and word quickly spread. After she had spent thirty thousand dollars redecorating her tiny gambling place in downtown Tokyo, people stopped coming. Then they stopped coming to the coffee shop too. With less and less money to count each night, her security collapsed, and depression overtook her. Keiko actually took to hiding behind the counter so she wouldn't have to face the customers. Her nights she spent crying. "You have a goal," she told Yoshi. "I never had a goal."

"I really liked my mother then," Yoshi said of those days. "I had never seen her humble before."

At that time, Yoshi worked at a trading company in downtown Tokyo, saving her money so she could leave Japan. To improve her English, she spent weekends at the local pizza parlor, where she took every opportunity to talk with the international clientele. She especially liked one particular sailor from the United States. "He was nice, and so different from other people who came in," Yoshi said. "He didn't drink like everyone else. And he wasn't in a rush to get married. He told me he was a Christian, but that didn't mean anything to me. I didn't know what a Christian was."

One day while Yoshi was at work, an old woman came in and introduced herself as Haru, her real grandmother. As Yoshi stared, Haru said she had come to take care of all three: Yoshi, Keiko and Granny Ai. "She was so kind, so gentle, but I was in shock to hear that Granny wasn't my real grandmother."

They had one day to pack everything and leave their house. As the three sat in the back seat of Haru's car, Yoshi held Granny Ai's hand to comfort her. At the new place, Yoshi shared a room with her ninety-year-old new grandmother, Haru. The old woman was very nice to her, but Yoshi was still determined to leave Japan. When she saw an advertisement for English studies at a state university in America, she persuaded her mother to let her go for six months.

Back at the pizza parlor, Yoshi exclaimed to the sailor—now her boyfriend—"I'm going to America! To Long Beach State University in California!"

Her boyfriend said he had a job with his brother in Modesto, California. Couldn't she find a school closer to Modesto? Yoshi did—San Jose State University.

"When I arrived in California, I finally felt free for the first time in my life," Yoshi said. "No more abuse! I didn't have to hear my mother yell at me every moment, telling me how dumb I was."

Every weekend her boyfriend came to visit. Sometimes Yoshi went to visit his family. When he suddenly suggested they marry, she said okay, even though neither of them had thought it through. She knew her mother would be furious.

An unforeseen consequence of getting married was that the university would not allow Yoshi to continue in school. Married women were barred from the program. Not yet fluent in English and knowing no one, she spent her days alone in their small apartment. Everything was new—language, culture, family. Even had she and her husband spoken the same language, she wouldn't have known how to communicate with him because she had never seen a healthy family interact. Fortunately, her brothers- and sisters-in-law were wonderful models and very kind to her, especially after she became pregnant.

"I watched them and I learned from them," she said. "I saw how they treated their children. My father-in-law was so accepting, and he never got angry. So my husband knew how to be a husband and a father. But I had so much baggage."

More than anything, Yoshi longed to be a good and loving mother. She had two sons, three years apart. As they grew into little boys, she began to worry: What would I do if something happened to my husband? I still can't speak English well enough to get a job. Over her husband's objections, she took a course preparing her to be a dental assistant. When the course was over, she was hired immediately. Once she started to work and talk to people all day, her English improved rapidly.

When Yoshi was thirty years old and her boys were approaching adolescence, she got a job that changed her life. It was with a dentist who was, in Yoshi's words, "like Christ." Almost all of his patients were also believers, and everyone had something about God to share with Yoshi.

"I hadn't planned to ever be a Christian," Yoshi said. Oh, she went to church on Sundays with her family, and she loved the music, but she couldn't understand the sermon. And she never even tried to read the Bible. Still, working in that dentist's office made her think about things in a whole new way.

When Yoshi married, she had promised her mother she would go back to Japan every three years to visit her. Yoshi dreaded those angry, guilt-filled trips, and she always came back home feeling miserable. One day when she telephoned, her mother answered in a strange voice. Yoshi knew immediately that something was very wrong. Even though it wasn't the appointed year, she would have to go to Japan and check on her.

On the plane over, Yoshi's usual anxiety froze into rock-hard fear. What if her mother came after her with a knife? What if she stabbed her in her sleep? For the first time, Yoshi prayed, "Oh, God, please protect me. I don't know what's going on, and I don't want to be hurt."

Yoshi found her mother sunk into a horrible depression, the worst ever. But instead of threatening her, Keiko said, "You are doing so well in America. It was good you went." Then, to Yoshi's amazement she added, "I want you to go visit your Granny Ai."

"Never in all my life had she spoken so kindly to me," Yoshi said. Then Yoshi understood. "It was because I had prayed to the real God."

On the way back to America, somewhere over the Pacific Ocean, Yoshi prayed, "Jesus, I want you to be my savior." As soon as she got home, she hurried to the church pastor's house. "I want to be a Christian!" she said. "And to get baptized too."

The women of the church surrounded Yoshi and mentored her. "I watched how they loved their husbands and how they treated them," she said. "How they overcame difficulties in their marriages. How they handled their teenagers. I didn't know how to be a good wife and mother. I had no idea how to live in harmony with my husband. I didn't want to abuse my kids like my mother had abused me, but sometimes I caught myself saying things that sounded like her. I have had to apologize to them many times."

Looking back, Yoshi says, "I was blessed to find Christ in American rather than Japan, because in Japan there are so few Christians that I would have had no one to mentor and teach me."

Yoshi began to think differently about her job too. Anyone with training could do what she did at the dentist's office. Some people were already doing it better than she. Surely there was a job out there that only she could do. "I was certain God didn't send me to America to be a dental assistant," Yoshi said. "He wanted me to serve him. But how?"

By ministering to Japanese people. She was certain that was what God wanted. But how? No other Japanese people lived in her small town. Who would lead the way for her?

But when God has a job for us, he shows us how to accomplish it.

A secular company in the area placed exchange students in local homes for two-week stays, and Yoshi volunteered to help. They were so desperate for homes that they would take anyone. Students told her horrendous stories, such as the girl who had to share a single bed with an eighty-nine-year-old woman. *I can do better than this!* Yoshi thought. *And I can place students in Christian homes where they can see the love of Jesus modeled.*

In 1995, Yoshi established Grace International Ministries (GMI) with the goal of ministering to exchange students. Not only did she spice up students' home stays with sightseeing outings and camping and ski trips, but the Christian host families truly embraced the young people, taking them along to church and youth groups. "It was eye-opening to the students that church could be so much fun," said Yoshi.

The first spring, Yoshi had five exchange-student girls. Two were already followers of Jesus. By the time the girls left, the other three were as well. Seven more came to the United States during the summer and they, too, were drawn to Christ through love.

Serving God in America was wonderful, but all Yoshi could think was, *What will happen to these new followers of Jesus Christ when they get back to Japan? Who will mentor them? How will they find a church?*

Yoshi didn't know of a single Christian church in any of Japan's big cities. But God knew. In 1999, a Japanese pastor contacted Yoshi and asked if she could arrange to have a missionary from America come to his church. It so happened that a woman named Kate had already contacted Yoshi about just such an opportunity. Kate went to Japan and moved into an apartment so tiny she could stand on her sleeping mat and touch everything in the room. But she was ecstatic. By six every morning, she was up and praying for the Japanese pastor and the church. With tears running down her cheeks, she prayed for each student by name.

"I felt ashamed," Yoshi said. "I never prayed and cried for Japan like that. I thought, *I want to be like her!* Kate was such an encouragement to the Japanese women.

"Japan isn't like America," Yoshi said. "People there are starving for the truth. When they meet a person like Kate, they are drawn to Jesus Christ."

Soon GMI was regularly sending missionaries to Japan to teach English as a Second Language (ESL) classes conducted through the few Japanese Christian churches there—a strikingly effective outreach to the communities.

Wherever there is terrible hurt, the opportunity for forgiveness exists. Looking back on her life, Yoshi says, "I love my mother, and I am sorry for the life she led. But the body God gave me is his temple, and I will no longer allow her to beat me. I have to lay down my boundaries. It has taken me years to come to the place of respecting myself enough to do this. But I do still go see her. If not me, who?"

Out of abuse, love.

Out of love, compassion.

Out of compassion, the gospel for Japan.

Step Out and Take Action
for Spiritual Life Change

*S*ince every person has a spiritual life, we simply do not believe it is valid to work at transforming a whole life and not offer life that goes on forever through Christ. Are you particularly compelled to have a part in moving people beyond "humanitarian" and into "eternal" change? If so, here are some beginning suggestions:

- Organize a prayer vigil specifically for the unreached areas in this book, and beyond. <JoshuaProject.net> offers current information on unreached people groups.

- Write a poem about how girls suffer without knowing God's love for them, and send it to us to put on our website.

- Sponsor a Sisters In Service exhibit at a church missions conference. Hand out our flyers about the lives of girls in unreached lands.

- Organize a local coalition of churches in your city to raise awareness, prayer and help for girls.

- Start a dinner club hosted in the homes of friends. The money you save from not going out to dinner can be invested in reaching girls with the good news of God's love.

- When you gather with other believers, suggest a moment of silence to pray for those who minister in countries that suppress the gospel. Tell the stories of Dorri and Nahid in Iran, Yoshi in Japan, Dorcas in Sudan, Grace in Timbuktu and so on.

- Organize your friends, book club or church to join the National Walk4Moms in May. The walk highlights the importance of women and girls, and benefits local and international programs that equip them for life now and forever. (For more information, go to <www .nationalwalk4moms.org>.)

- Give a gift that matches what you spend to develop spiritually (money for books, Bible study materials, driving to events, retreats, church).

- Light a candle every night at dinner, and pray for unreached girls to experience the light of God's love.

Conclusion

Looking Through Eyes of Hope

*E*arthquakes, hurricanes, tsunamis, cyclones. Natural disasters strike without warning, killing thousands and wiping out entire towns. Shocked and saddened, we mourn the victims even as we rally to help survivors pick up their lives and move on. Yet we tend to accept such catastrophes as inevitable. Nature at work. Just a part of life.

What makes no sense at all are the disasters we humans bring on ourselves: health plagues that could be avoided with clean water, sanitation and medication; generations of suffering because entire villages have no access to education; sexual slavery that flourishes because laws are not enforced; childhoods stolen because child labor and exploitation have huge financial benefits and few challenges; war because the powerful crave still more power.

To these tragedies, our common response is to shake our heads and cluck our tongues and ask, "What is this world coming to?"

How is it that although we in the West know about these horrific situations, they fail to pull us together into actually getting busy and doing something? Why is that?

Eager for an answer, Kay stood on street corners in several American cities and posed this question to passersby: "Why do you think we Americans are more hesitant to help the victims of man-made disasters, such as sex trafficking of children, than the victims of natural disasters, such as earthquakes or tsunamis?"

In this admittedly unscientific survey, four top answers (or variations thereof) emerged:

1. Those are other countries' problems. It's not our business. We have poor and hurting people in our own country.

2. Relief groups are already taking care of those issues.

3. I would like to be involved, but I don't know what to do.

4. I'm just one person. I can't make a difference.

Our short response to those answers: "It absolutely is our business! We are citizens of the same world, after all. If relief groups really were already 'taking care of' the issues, then the problems wouldn't still be with us—and growing. Oh, and stick around because we have great suggestions on how you can get involved and really make a difference!"

But don't stop reading yet. Each of these questions deserves a more complete answer.

Answer 1: Those are other countries' problems. We realize that the two of us have a big advantage over the average person on the street, perhaps even over most people sitting in church on Sundays. We have done a tremendous amount of research. We know, for instance, that studies show that people in the United States focused over 90 percent of their charitable giving right here in our own country. In this country and in many areas of the Western world, we enforce laws that protect the weak, and we also have social services and strong churches to help the needy. This isn't true in most of the places we address in this book.

Also, we have had the privilege of talking directly to girls who live under oppression and with so few of life's necessities. We have seen their hopelessness, but we have also watched when they first began to realize their possibilities.

But here is the point: what we in our country take for granted should move us with gratitude to intervene for our sisters around the world. No one should have to risk her life every time she drinks a cup of water. No one should be so shackled by illiteracy that marriage at the age of ten seems like a good option—or the only option. No one should ever live such an existence that selling their child to a sex trafficker looks like the right thing to do.

There are many things we in the West could learn from our sisters and brothers in the hard parts of the world: perseverance and endurance and resilience and patience and adaptability and unity, to name a few.

But some things we know quite well. We know, for instance, that educating girls is the strongest lever for their empowerment. We know that education goes a long way toward helping to reduce poverty. We know that it also opens up an array of options for girls and young women who previously thought their only hope was to get a husband, any husband, at any cost. We know, too, that education can help change social norms, such as the practice of ridding the family of "worthless" girls.

Another thing we know is how important it is that people have access to clean water and proper sanitation. We know that when an area has these critical necessities of life, children's health improves dramatically. We know that instead of burying their babies, mothers are able to watch them grow and thrive.

The problem is that many mothers in the hardest places of the world don't know these things. And so they keep their girls home from school and send them instead to the nearest water hole to scoop up polluted water for the family's use.

Can anyone truly say this is not our business?

Oh, and we know something else. One humanitarian improvement automatically leads to the next and then the next, and so the benefits combine and multiply.

In North Africa, we visited a village that had just received a well with a water pump. No longer did the girls have to spend hours walking to and from the river, balancing heavy water jars on their heads. Water toting had always been their job, just as it had been the job of their mothers before them and their grandmothers before that. But now, with so much free time, well, why not let the girls go to school?

So two days a week the district teacher came to their village. And the girls attended school, many with small brothers or sisters tied to their backs. (They no longer had to carry water, but they were still needed as babysitters. More than ever, in fact, for the survival rate of babies soared once they had clean water.) The children learned to read and write, but they also learned other things, such as the importance of washing their hands, as well as their pots and pans, before they used them to eat. Never before had anyone dared waste water on such a frivolous pastime as washing! But since the washing started, mothers noticed that their children were sick much less frequently. So everyone washed—the old people and the toddlers too.

The village head man told us, "We thank you for showing us the love of God by giving us clean water."

The village got a well, and look what happened:

- The village had water.
- Far more babies were surviving.
- Their animals survived in times of drought.
- For the first time, girls were learning to read and write.
- Basic sanitation methods were bringing greater health to the village.
- The girls saw a woman, their teacher, model new life options.
- The villagers saw and acknowledged the love of God in action.

All for the price of a well.

Imagine the combined long-range effects of many interventions in many different areas. If the neediest girls can be equipped to lead lives free of abuse and enabled to move forward empowered with opportunities and hope for the future, their influence on the next generation will include even greater possibilities. Their daughters will grow up knowing they have a future.

Answer 2: Relief groups are already taking care of those issues. Without a doubt, relief groups are addressing these issues, and many are doing the job quite well. While some are primarily aimed at providing relief during times of disaster and then moving on to the next disaster in the next place, other groups do both relief and development work.

It is this second phase—development—that is so essential for the long term. And it must be done wisely and with great sensitivity and understanding. We see it accomplished most successfully by small-scale, local interveners, even those with meager resources, that are on hand during every disaster. Local people build deep relationships before a crisis arises, they are there to assist throughout the crisis, and they are there to help long after the world's eyes have been turned elsewhere. For instance, when we look at the people sharing blankets and food with widows and orphans in Darfur today, and the ones providing vocational training for their neighbors and schools for their children, we see that they are local Christians who were themselves displaced. No one has to tell them what is needed. They know from experience. Working together with these existing organizations gives us a ready-made opportunity to help find long-term solutions.

Long-term solutions include

- giving a voice to the voiceless
- building relationships
- working together with local initiatives
- offering viable alternatives to the way things have always been done

By working together, we can do much to extend God's love.

In Nepal, we were touched by the plight of Dona, a widow at twenty-six. Her husband died of AIDS, but by the time she knew what made him sick, she and her two children were already infected. So here Dona was, a young widow dying of AIDS, totally stigmatized in her community, constantly sick with every opportunistic bug that came her way. She had two young children, five and seven, who were not allowed to go to school or to play with other children or even to go to the well to draw water. What could we possibly do to help her? Even more, what could we do to change the circumstances that caused her situation and fed her distress: ignorance as to what causes AIDS, poverty, lack of medical care?

Nothing, you say? Well, in one way that answer is right, but in another way it is wrong.

It's true that we are not right there in Nepal to care for Dona and her children. We cannot transport her to the hospital every month for treatments. We cannot force the school to accept her little ones or to persuade the parents that their children are in no danger from playing with them. We cannot lecture the villagers on HIV/AIDS infection. We cannot even share the eternal hope of heaven with Dona.

But we are far from helpless. God's "interveners" are present in the mountains of Nepal, and they are already working at all these things and more, because a persistent Nepalese Christian woman has earned the respect of highly placed government officials. Unfortunately, in the face of such opportunity, local resources are in terribly short supply. So the best way for us to help Dona is to raise awareness in our country, then pull together a variety of resources that can strengthen the local hands already at work in Nepal.

Answer 3: I'd like to be involved, but I don't know what to do. This was an encouraging answer, because Kay had suggestions ready to whip out and hand people right there on the street corner where she was doing the survey. Of course, what she heard in response was, "Uh, well, maybe later. I'm pretty busy right now, but, um . . ."

Unfortunately "I don't know what to do" can mean "I know I should act, and I feel guilty for not doing it, but I'm afraid I won't like what you ask me to do." But for many, this answer is completely sincere. And even if you happen to be one of the more hesitant, you may be surprised to find a perfect way to get started through the following plans of action:

Get the facts. When people don't know the condition of the worlds' girls, they are not as likely to feel inspired to take action. Marci, who read the manuscript for this book, was inspired to continue reading and digging, then she came back and said, "I discovered that a lot of the child labor abuses are encouraged by us. I like cheap clothes just as much as the next guy, but from now on, before I buy I'm going to ask how and where the cheap stuff is made. I am determined to be a responsible consumer."

Where might you make changes in your life that will make a difference for hurting girls?

Speak on behalf of the voiceless. Maureen has never been to Timbuktu, and it's doubtful she will ever go. She isn't much of a traveler, and she does have a hip replacement to deal with (it always sets off the airport alarm). But mention Africa to Maureen and you had better pull up a chair. She will tell you all about the women's center there. Then just when you think she surely does need to take a breath, her passion for empowering castoff girls will spill out all over again: "Training and microloans—they can actually change lives. And they cost less than you probably spend on coffee each month. What a bargain! Why, without a microloan . . ."

Maureen knows what she's talking about. She has made it her business to know. She has pictures, she has figures, and she has evidence of concrete results.

Were you to hear from a young African mother living in an outlying village in Timbuktu, she would probably plead for some way to earn money to feed her children. But how are you going to hear from a mother in Timbuktu? It's likely you will hear from someone like Maureen who speaks on that mother's behalf.

Like Maureen, you too can be the voice for someone who is not being heard.

Give money. Yes, we know. Many people want to be involved in ways other than giving money. But let's face the bottom line: it costs to get things done. And giving is often truly the best way to help— not just giving, but giving wisely and knowledgeably.

Remember Dona in Nepal? The chain of help wound from her

to the ministry in the Himalayas, across the ocean to Sisters In Service in the United States, but then it came as an invitation to the people with resources. That would be us, the fortunate ones who say "I'm starving" when we only mean "I'm ready for yet another meal today," or "I haven't got a thing to wear" when we mean "I'm tired of all my clothes so I think I'll go shopping and buy some new ones." That's us—the people God has chosen to entrust with so much, but only as his stewards, because it all belongs to him.

You can't do everything, and neither can we. No one can. But every one of us can do something. We can use the power of the purse and the power of prayer to invest in a stronger future for abused and exploited girls.

Pray knowledgeably. "Dear God, bless everyone in need and everyone who is hungry. Amen."

Hmm. That is a mighty limp prayer. Not that God isn't capable of sorting it out and answering it, but what does such weak praying do for you? Now consider an alternative; let's use the plight of Majeeda in Pakistan as an example. Pray for her urgently and in detail, and you will automatically be drawn to listen to reports concerning attacks on Christians in Pakistan. When that issue is covered in *Time Magazine,* you will read it carefully, because you know someone there.

As you continue to learn, your prayers will grow more urgent. When the opportunity comes to write to your lawmakers on behalf of Christians struggling under the oppressive laws in Pakistan, you will be one of the first to do so, because you already have a personal interest. You have "family" there. You will pray for our lawmakers, too, that they will be convicted to use their influence.

Do you see what is happening? Your knowledgeable and faithful prayer is changing you.

And not only you, for the Bible says, "You do not have, because you do not ask God" (James 4:2). Your faithful, knowledgeable prayers will also change those you are praying for.

Answer 4: I'm just one person; I can't really make a difference. One woman in Nepal is rescuing girls from sex traffickers because one woman in Britain shared her vision and gave her the financial support to begin.

One woman in Hong Kong is spreading God's Word throughout southern China because almost thirty years ago one woman in Wisconsin paid for her to go to school.

One couple in California prayed for a pastor and his wife in Bangladesh. Their prayers led them to share with their Bible study group, which led to full-time support for the pastor and his wife, which led to countless new believers in a harsh land.

One businessman donates his time to speak to men's groups about the plight of exploited girls, and more girls are rescued because of his efforts.

One woman in Maine made a commitment to pray every day for a woman in India and her three girls. All three daughters went through school and are serving God as teachers and the wives of pastors, two in the difficult state of Orissa.

One woman found a way to point the resistant people of Japan to God through their eagerness to learn English.

One junior-high student in Pennsylvania read sections of *Daughters of Hope* to her friends, and they all baked and sold cookies until they had enough to pay for a well in a village in West Africa.

One woman from Alabama started the first-ever mission program in her poverty-stricken church by encouraging church members to save just a few dollars a month for a project in Africa.

One woman from Washington plucked up her courage and traveled to Egypt, and then she returned home as a powerful advocate for the struggling Christians there.

What can God do through one dedicated person?

Only change the world!

GOD SAYS . . .

When Jesus walked on the earth, he looked out over the multitudes of needy people. Yet he never shook his head, clucked his tongue or joined the others of his day in saying, "What is this world coming to?" Oh no. Moved with compassion, he prayed for them. He healed the sick, he fed the hungry, and he told the multitudes of his Father God's love. He asked the Lord of the harvest for more laborers of all kinds.

Jesus set aside his own riches in heaven, and he came to earth to pay a debt he did not owe. It cost him his life, but out of that horror rose our great hope of life eternal.

In this natural world, we will not see an end to injustice and oppression. But that should never stop us from reaching toward what should be. First of all, it is the right thing to do. Even more, it is what God requires of us.

> He has shown you, O man, what is good.
>> And what does the LORD require of you?
> To act justly and to love mercy
>> and to walk humbly with your God. (Micah 6:8)

The time will come when all will be set right. One day God will redeem every horror that now seems absolutely unredeemable. We know this is true, because he already turned the darkest day in human history into the greatest of all hopes.

But until that day of redemption, it is our responsibility and our privilege to embrace the least of our sisters and brothers, to strengthen the weak, to raise up the oppressed, to speak out for the voiceless. We have the glad opportunity to move beyond our own preoccupations with ourselves and to work on behalf of the most vulnerable in the hardest places, and from them to learn lessons of perseverance and humility and gratitude.

It is for us to look out at the desert through eyes of hope and to rejoice over every beautiful blossom.

Appendix

Recommended Reading

*F*ollowing is a list of the best research and literature from the most current and reliable sources we know. However, we do not intend to imply that we necessarily agree with or support the perspectives of the organizations represented here.

PART 1: PHYSICAL LIFE

Hesketh, Therese, and Zhu Wei Xing. "Abnormal Sex Ratios in Human Populations: Causes and Consequences." Edited by Jeremy Nathans. Proceedings of the National Academy of Sciences of the United States of America. 17 July 2006. <www.pnas.org/content/103/36/13271.full>

> Through female infanticide and discrimination in the care of young girls, India and China have eighty million "missing" females. A disproportionate number of males are reaching maturity, which causes problems that could threaten the stability of these societies. This article recommends the necessary measures to bring about balance, including enforcement of legislation, equal rights for women and education on gender imbalance.

Owen, Dean. "India: Girls Sacrificed to Tradition: Former Religious Prostitutes Help Those Still Trapped." World Vision eNews. <www.worldvision.org/about_us.nsf/child/eNews_india_051606>

> As many as five thousand Indian girls are "married" to a god at a young age and become temple prostitutes every year. Many of them have been told that they cannot say no to any man, and they contract HIV. World Vision works to rescue these prostitutes.

Family Care International (FCI) and United Nations Population Fund (UNFPA). "Living Testimony: Obstetric Fistula and Inequities in Maternal Health." Campaign to End Fistula. 2007. <www.endfistula.org/download/living%20testimony_english.pdf>

> This gives information about fistula and its causes, as well as vignettes from those who have it and/or have been treated for it.

Pande, Rohini, and Anju Malhotra. "Son Preference and Daughter Neglect in India: What Happens to Living Girls." International Center for Research on Women. 2006. <www.icrw.org/docs/2006_son-prefer ence.pdf>

> This study found that the single most important factor for reducing son preference is education of the mother. In addition, the preference for sons is not universal but does cross economic barriers. Finally girls with older sisters are more likely to be neglected than girls with older brothers.

Jones, Adam. "Case Study: Female Infanticide." Gendercide Watch. 1 October 2007. <www.gendercide.org/case_infanticide.html>

> A short article discussing female infanticide, most specifically in India and China. It includes case studies and statistics.

Rickett, Daniel, and Michele Rickett. *Least Valued No More: Research and Recommendations on the Plight of Women and Girls.* Roswell, Ga.: Sisters In Service, 2008.

"Looking into the cases and statistics concerning suffering women and girls is a first step in the journey to making wise decisions for intervention. . . . It is our privilege to introduce you to the most current findings, along with best practical solutions for the least-reached and least-valued human beings in our troubled world." Much of the research cited in the introduction of *Forgotten Girls* is drawn from this book.

"Every Day, 1400 Girls and Women Die Giving Birth: On Women's Day, UNICEF Says Lack of Progress is Shameful." UNICEF press release. 7 March 2003. <www.unicef.org/media/media_7594.html>

A UNICEF press release, this reveals facts about the staggering numbers of girls and women who die giving birth. It also discusses HIV and the exploitation of girls and women.

"Calling for an End to Female Genital Mutilation/Cutting." United Nations Population Fund. <www.unfpa.org/gender/practices1.htm>

An informative, easy-to-read article, this describes Female Genital Mutilation/Cutting (FGMC) and the short- and long-term impact it has on girls and women.

"Massive Campaign Across the Country Needed to Fight Female Foeticide: Cecilio Adorna." UNICEF India. <www.unicef.org/india/children_2745.htm>

This is an interview with Ceclio Adorna, UNICEF representative in India.

PART 2: EDUCATIONAL LIFE
"How School Transformed a Girl's Life—and Helped Her Village Too." UNICEF Egypt. <www.unicef.org/egypt/reallives_161.html>

"Girls' Education: A World Bank Priority." World Bank. <http://go.worldbank.org/1L4BH3TG20>

This article discusses the importance of a girl's education and includes good statistics.

"The Barriers to Educating Girls." UNICEF. <www.unicef.org/girls-education/index_barriers.html>

A short article, this discusses some of the barriers to educating girls.

PART 3: SEXUAL PROTECTION FOR LIFE

"Child Trafficking." UNICEF. <www.unicef.org/protection/exploitation.html>

This short article by UNICEF includes statistics about child trafficking.

The Child Trafficking Research Hub of UNICEF offers some helpful resources, although not much is gender specific: <www.childtrafficking.org/>.

PART 4: FREEDOM IN LIFE

"Photo Op: Child Brides in Afghanistan," an interview with Stephanie Sinclair. National Public Radio. 7 July 2006. <www.npr.org/templates/player/mediaPlayer.html?action=1&t=1&islist=false&id=5541006&m=5541007> (The photographs are hosted at <www.npr.org/templates/story/story.php?storyId=5541006>.)

This three-minute National Public Radio segment details pictures taken by Stephanie Sinclair. Pictures capture the lack of freedom well. The interview was also helpful in describing some of Sinclair's experience.

Stritof, Sheri and Bob Stritof. "Child Brides: The Problem of Early, Forced Marriage." About.com. <http://marriage.about.com/od/arrangedmarriages/a/childbride.htm>

A short, straightforward article about child brides, this includes statistics on ages and prevalence around the world.

"When Marriage Is No Haven . . . Child Marriage in Developing Countries: What Works to Keep Girls Safe." International Center for Research on Women. September 2004. <www.icrw.org/docs/2004_info_childmarriage.pdf>

> This includes statistics related to the effects of girls marrying young as well as suggestions for what works to help combat child marriage. It includes several different articles through the International Center for Research on Women.

Ayotte, Barbara. "Burmese and Hill Tribe Women and Girls Without Status in Thailand at Unaddressed Risk of Human Rights Abuses and HIV/AIDS." Physicians for Human Rights. 14 July 2004. <http://physiciansforhumanrights.org/library/news-2004-07-14.html>

> This article discusses abuses of girls in Thailand, including the lack of status for women and girls, rape of girls, exploitation and more.

PART 5: SPIRITUAL LIFE

Sheikh, Bilquis, and Richard H. Schneider. *I Dared to Call Him Father: The Miraculous Story of a Muslim Woman's Encounter with God.* Grand Rapids: Baker, 2003.

> "At a time when new questions about Islam arise daily, the miraculous story of Bilquis Sheikh will help Christians understand and reach out to Muslims with compassion and the gospel. A wealthy Pakistani woman, the outspoken Sheikh came to know God through a dream, turning her world upside down, putting her life in danger."

Strom, Kay Marshall, and Michele Rickett. *Daughters of Hope: Stories of Witness and Hope in the Face of Persecution.* Downers Grove, Ill.: InterVarsity Press, 2003.

> "Throughout the world today, Christians continue to face intense persecution, and Christian women are often the most vulnerable. In Pakistan, Christian girls are systematically kidnapped, tortured

and raped. In China, underground church leaders are sent to labor camps for hosting illegal home meetings. In Sudan, Christian women are captured and sold into slavery or mutilated and left to die. And in many Muslim countries, a woman can be killed by her husband or father for converting to Christianity. In this deeply moving book, Kay Marshall Strom and Michele Rickett tell the stories of persecuted Christian women from around the world. From Africa to the Middle East to Asia, they give voice to our sisters persevering under the yoke of oppression and injustice."

Companien, Anneke. *Singing Through the Night: Courageous Stories of Faith from Women in the Persecuted Church.* Grand Rapids: Revell, 2007.

"There are many untold stories of the persecuted church—stories of women who bravely follow Christ at any cost. This stirring book reveals the lives of eleven women in nine different countries around the world. They have lost husbands, children, homes, jobs, or their very freedom and yet continue to praise and serve the Lord. The lessons that these courageous women learned in tough times will help you persevere and endure whatever hardships come your way."

Companien, Anneke. *Hidden Sorrow, Lasting Joy: The Forgotten Women of the Persecuted Church.* Wheaton, Ill.: Tyndale House, 2001.

"These are the stories of twenty women from around the world— all wives of men who are Christian martyrs or have been imprisoned for their faith. The women are from such places as Vietnam, China and Iran. These amazing and inspiring stories will help readers focus their prayers and raise awareness of this often hidden subject."

Ilibagiza, Immaculée. *Left to Tell: Discovering God Amidst the Rwandan Holocaust.* Carlsbad, Calif.: Hay House, 2007.

"In 1994, Rwandan native Ilibagiza was twenty-two years old and home from college to spend Easter with her devout Catholic family, when the death of Rwanda's Hutu president sparked a three-month slaughter of nearly one million ethnic Tutsis in the country. She survived by hiding in a Hutu pastor's tiny bathroom with seven other starving women for ninety-one cramped, terrifying days. This searing firsthand account of Ilibagiza's experience cuts two ways: her description of the evil that was perpetrated, including the brutal murders of her family members, is soul-numbingly devastating, yet the story of her unquenchable faith and connection to God throughout the ordeal uplifts and inspires. . . . Ilibagiza's remarkable path to forgiving the perpetrators and releasing her anger is a beacon to others who have suffered injustice."

FOR FURTHER READING

<www.compassdirect.org>
News from the frontlines of persecution

<http://hrw.org>
Human Rights Watch
Click on the "Women's Rights" topic for information about protecting women around the world.

International Center for Research on Women

<www.unicef.org>
United Nations Children's Fund

<www.worldvision.org>
World Vision

Photo Credits and Descriptions

Photos taken by Sisters In Service staff unless otherwise noted.

Introduction
Indian toddler (photographer: Amber Warner)

Chapter 1: Stand Up to the Witch
Indonesian girl with bobbed hair

Chapter 2: Disposable Mothers
Tent dwelling

Chapter 3: Sacrificed to Gods
Indian toddler

Chapter 4: Not Enough Girls
Chinese girl in a thicket (photographer: Peggy Wales)

Chapter 5: Education for AIDS Orphans
Chinese girl with certificate

Chapter 6: Beautiful Music From Untouchable Girls
Indian girl in pinned-together, blue dress
(photographer: Kay Marshall Strom)

Chapter 7: Given by the Chief
Two Senegalese girls

Chapter 8: A New Way
Egyptian girl behind a door (photographer: Kay Marshall Strom)

Chapter 9: Temporary Wives in Timbuktu
Malian village girl

Chapter 10: Kidnapped!
Teen Kyrgyz girl

Chapter 11: Girls for Sale
Group of Nepali children

Chapter 12: Throwaway Girls
Indian toddler

Chapter 13: Behind Prison Bars
Pakistan girls at risk (photo courtesy of Jubilee Campaign
<www.jubileecampaign.org>)

Chapter 14: Surviving War
Sudan teen girl in the classroom, with boys in the background

Chapter 15: Sisters of War
Iraqi girl with headdress

Chapter 16: An Awakening
Iranian girl in scarf (photo courtesy of ELAM ministries
<www.elam.com>; the mission of ELAM is to strengthen and
expand the church in the Iran region and beyond)

Chapter 17: From Daughter of a Geisha to Daughter of the King
Japanese child and grandmother (photo courtesy of Yoshiko Hanks)

Notes

page 18   In the most-affected areas, five: "Every Day, 1400 Girls and
              Women Die Giving Birth," UNICEF press release, <www
              .unicef.org/media/media_7594.html>.

page 18   According to UNICEF, gender-based infanticide: "Child Pro-
              tection from Violence, Exploitation, and Abuse," UNICEF,
              2 October 2007 <www.unicef.org/protection/index_
              discrimination.html>.

page 42   Yet we do have quiet ways of helping: *Postscript:* An April
              2008 Compass Direct News article cites the U.S. Commis-
              sion on International Religious Freedom's (USCIRF) report
              from the same month.

              The Chinese government continues to forcibly repatriate
              North Koreans who have entered China without proper au-
              thorization back to North Korea, where they face brutal inter-
              rogations, detentions, forced labor, and they often disappear
              into the infamous *kwanliso* or political penal labor colonies.

              The report reiterates that the freedom to leave one's coun-
              try of origin is a right protected by both the Universal Decla-
              ration on Human Rights and the International Covenant on
              Civil and Political Rights. North Korea is a party to the latter,
              yet it is illegal to leave North Korea without authorization.

              The report calls on the international community to press
              China to cease repatriating North Korean refugees and pro-
              vide protection for them as required by the 1951 Convention
              and its 1967 Protocols, to which China is a party.

              In January 2009, the ministry Open Doors released its
              annual World Watch List of the worst religious persecu-
              tors, with North Korea topping the list for the sixth con-
              secutive year.

page 45   The "State of the World's Mothers 2005" report: Save the
              Children, "State of the World's Mothers 2005: The Power

and Promise of Girls' Education," May 2005, <www.savethe
children.org/publications/mothers/2005/SOWM_2005.pdf>,
p. 4.

page 46   According to a report by the World Bank: "Gender Equality
and the Millennium Development Goals," World Bank Gen-
der and Development Group, April 4, 2003, <http://site
resources.worldbank.org/INTGENDER/Publications/
20706126 /gendermdg.pdf>, p. 7.

page 50   An estimated 140,000 Chinese: UNICEF China, 2007
Report.

page 51   By 2010 as many as ten million Chinese: 10 Million AIDS
cases in China by 2010, "2004 Report on the Global AIDS
Epidemic UNAIDS" (Joint United Nations Programme on
HIV/AIDS), p. 6.

page 73   Only 44 percent say they: Fatma El-Zanaty, *Egypt Demo-
graphic and Health Survey 1995* (Calverton, Md.: Macro International, 1996).

page 82   In 2001 alone, an estimated twelve thousand girls: "Nepal
HIV/AIDS Among Prostitutes," The World Bank Report, *HIV/
AIDS in South Asia,* August 2008, p. 2.

page 92   According to the British Broadcasting: Lonely Planet.

page 95   In his documentary film: See an interview with Peter Lom
and his *Frontline* video at <www.pbs.org/frontlineworld/
stories/kyrgyzstan/thestory.html>.

page 101   A recent UNICEF study estimates: UNICEF 2002 Report,
"Unbearable to the Human Heart: Child Trafficking and Action to Eliminate It," p. 28.

page 105   2.8 million prostitutes: Ministry of Women and Child Development, Government of India.

page 105   Under age eighteen: "Around 2.8 Million Prostitutes in India," *Indian Express Newpaper,* May 8, 2007.

page 105   According to a survey: Surana Pawan, *Effect of Globalisation
on Human Trafficking and Forced Prostitution,* p. 2.

page 112   Sanction-related causes in Iraq: UNICEF, United Nations.

page 112   "Lord's Resistance Army": BBC News, "Uganda Conflict
'Worse than Iraq,'" November 2003.

page 112   Fifteen thousand Liberian: "Watch List on Children and
Armed Conflict," <www.watchlist.org>.

page 112   Uganda and the Republic of Congo: Jina Moore, "In Africa Justice for 'Bush Wives,'" *Christian Science Monitor,* June 8, 2008.

page 112   In Iraq, schools: UNICEF 2003 IRQ: Iraq Watching Briefs—Overview Report, July 2003.

page 112   Data shows that of all war-affected: "Children and Armed Conflict," Office of the Special Representative of the Secretary-General, <www.un.org/children/conflict/english/girls inwar.html>.

page 115   Lowest female literacy rates: Regional Rural Sociologist/Women in Development Officer, "Food and Agriculture Organization of the United Nations (FAO) Report on Pakistan," p. 1.

page 115   Close to three-quarters of the female detainees: Lys Anzia, "Women's Prisons—A Global State of Crisis," Women News Network, <www.womennewsnetwork.net/2008/09/09/prison crisiswomen9005/>.

page 138   Morality houses: Dr. Donna M. Hughes, "Sex Slave Jihad," FrontPageMagazine.com, January 2004.

page 138   "There has been a 635 percent": Ibid.

SISTERS IN SERVICE

STRENGTHEN THE WEAK
SATISFY THE OPPRESSED
SPEAK UP FOR THE VOICELESS

EQUIPPING THE LEAST VALUED

Sisters In Service tackles the hardest-hitting issues women and girls face with empowering programs of education, health and vocational training, micro-loans, discipleship, rescue and restoration led by local Christian women.

We need people who will stand with us in prayer and financial support to continue to press against the privations and abuses women and girls face.

JOIN THE RESISTANCE AGAINST ABUSE AND EXPLOITATION OF GIRLS

Resist the Darkness™ is the SIS program that mobilizes people and provides practical interventions for girls who have been abused, abandoned, abducted, enslaved. . . . Join the resistance today, and start intervening and changing the lives of little girls now and forever.

Become a Resist the Darkness™ Champion personally by going to our website <www.SistersInService.org> and clicking on "Get Involved/Resist the Darkness." Follow the prompts to register as RTD Champion. You can help to start a Resist the Darkness™ Task Force with your friends or church. We will give you everything you need and coach you to mobilize people and resources. You will receive a picture of a girl from one of our areas of ministry, with prayer information throughout the year. The President's Audio Update will come to you via e-mail once a month.

We have written that you can contact us for more information, and we really mean it. We would love to hear how this book has touched and motivated you. We will help you raise your voice in any way we can.

If you'd like to book Michele or Kay to come and speak about *Forgotten Girls* or other topics, you can contact us at <kay@kaystrom.com> or <mrickett@SistersInService.org>.

---

*The goal of Sisters In Sevice (SIS) is
to mobilize a passionate, organized outcry
on behalf of the least valued human beings
on the planet: women and girls—
while intervening with help
to equip and empower them.*

*We work to see practical
and eternal life change in as many
women and girls as possible.*

Michele Rickett
Founder/President